Irish Books and Irish People

IRISH BOOKS
AND IRISH PEOPLE

By

STEPHEN LUCIUS GWYNN

Essay Index Reprint Series

BOOKS FOR LIBRARIES PRESS
FREEPORT, NEW YORK

First Published 1920
Reprinted 1969

STANDARD BOOK NUMBER:
8369-1136-9

LIBRARY OF CONGRESS CATALOG CARD NUMBER:
74-86756

PRINTED IN THE UNITED STATES OF AMERICA

Contents

	Page
INTRODUCTION	1
NOVELS OF IRISH LIFE IN THE NINETEENTH CENTURY	7
A CENTURY OF IRISH HUMOUR	23
LITERATURE AMONG THE ILLITERATES :	
I.—THE SHANACHY	44
II.—THE LIFE OF A SONG	51
IRISH EDUCATION AND IRISH CHARACTER	65
THE IRISH GENTRY	83
YESTERDAY IN IRELAND	97

INTRODUCTION.

Y publisher must take at least some of the responsibility for reviving these essays. All bear the marks of the period at which they were written; and some of them deal with the beginnings of movements which have since grown to much greater strength, and in growing have developed new characteristics at the expense of what was originally more prominent. Other pages, again, take no account of facts which to-day must be present to the mind of every Irish reader, and so are, perhaps significantly, out of date.   Nobody for instance, could now complain that Irish humour is lacking in seriousness.   Synge disposed of that criticism—and, indeed, the Abbey Theatre in its tone as a whole may ·be accused of neglecting Ireland's gift for simple fun.   Yet Lady Gregory made the most of it in her " Spreading the News," and Mr. Yeats in his " Pot of Broth."—How beautifully W. G. Fay interpreted an Irish laughter which had no bitterness in it.

But the strong intellectual movement which has swept over Ireland has been both embittering and embittered.   These last five and twenty years have been the most formative in the country's history of any since Ireland became the composite nation that she now is, or, perhaps, has yet to become.   At the back of it all lies the great social change involved in the transfer of ownership from the landlord to the cultivators of the soil—a change which has literally disenserfed three-fourths of Ireland's people. Yet the relations are obscure, indefinite, and intangible, which unite that material result to the outcome of two forces, allied but distinct, which have operated solely on men's minds and spirits. These are, of course, the Gaelic revival and the whole literary movement which has had its most concrete expression in the Irish theatre, and its most potent inspiration in the personality of Mr. Yeats.

Of these two forces, one can show by far the more tangible effects, for the Gaelic League has issued in action. Setting out to revive and save the Irish language as a living speech, the instrument of a nation's intercourse, it has failed of its purpose; but it has revived and rendered potent the principle of separation. Nationalist, it will have nothing to do with a nationality that is not as plainly marked off from other nationalities as a red lamp from a green lamp; and the essential symbol of separate nationality is for orthodox Gaelic Leaguers a separate language. America, said an able exponent of this doctrine the other day in a public debate, will never and never can be a nation till its language is no longer recognisable as English—till its English differs as much from the language of England as German differs from Dutch. An inevitable corollary to this view is the necessity for complete political separation from Great Britain—if only to provide the machinery for this complete differentiation by daily speech.

I cannot pretend to assess impartially the value of this movement. It asserted itself in passionate deeds at a moment when many thousands of us Nationalists were taking equally vigorous action in pursuit of a less tribal ideal. Thousands of us lost our lives, all of us risked our lives, with the hope of achieving a national unity which could never be built on the basis of regarding no man as an Irishman who did not speak, or at least desire to speak, Gaelic for his mother tongue. The action of Irish soldiers was thwarted and frustrated by the action of a very few separatists, with a very small expense to themselves in bloodshed. But the tribute to the work of the Gaelic League is that Ireland accepted them and rejected us. None can deny that it has been a potent stimulus to national education; and it only lacks official prohibition by the British Government to become more powerful still.

Whatever the outcome, I take back nothing of what is written in these papers concerning the Gaelic revival. In a country governed against the will of its people, forces that, under normal and healthy conditions, would be purely beneficent, may easily grow explosive and disruptive. Yet I have not changed my mind on a critical question which led me to sever my connection with the work of the Gaelic League. When that body decided to rely on compulsion rather than persuasion, it took the wrong road, if its object was to endear the Irish language to all Ireland, and to induce all Irishmen to cherish it as part of the common national heritage. As a result Ulstermen have a perfect right to say that if they accepted Home Rule, one of the first steps of an Irish government formed under the present auspices would be to demand a knowledge of Gaelic as the necessary qualification for holding any public office.

I do not believe that this tribal idealism which is

now so potent will endure. It is out of harmony with
the world's development—a world which in order to
preserve the very principle of small nationalities, is
growing more and more international. America is
not only a nation, but is the type of the modern nation
—bound together less by what it inherits from the
past, than by what it hopes from the future.

The other force which has been operating through
these years is, in a sense, obliged to give the lie to the
pretensions of the Gaelic League. Yeats and Synge
have showed how completely it is possible to be Irish
while using the English language. They have accepted
the fact that Ireland to-day thinks in English, but they
have endeavoured to give to Ireland a distinctively
Irish thought, coloured by the whole racial tradition
and temperament. With them has been allied
a personality not less Irish, yet less obviously
Irish—" A. E.," George Russell. Between them,
these writers and thinkers have profoundly
influenced the mind of the generation younger
than themselves. It is not possible to deny
that Ireland's literary output during those last twenty
years is far more important and serious than that of the
whole preceding century. The only part of it exempt
from these influences is the work of Edith Somerville
and Martin Ross; and even that is based on a closer
study of distinctively Irish speech than had ever been
attempted in earlier days. The propagandist work of
Pearse and Arthur Griffiths—equal in merit to that of
their forerunners, Davis and Mitchel—was Irish only
in substance and spirit, not in form or accent—a thing
the less surprising, since both men were only half Irish
by parentage. But the whole group of writers, of whom

it may be said that their writings are almost as unmistakably Irish as the work of Burns is Scotch, have
followed Mr. Yeats and Synge in this, that in writing
they assume an Irish public, not an English one; they
make no explanations, they speak as to those who
share their own inheritance.   In this group has been
fostered a spirit of the freedom which belongs properly
to art. Thus the school, for it may justly be called a
school, has created its own tradition, and it has been
a tradition of freedom, not asserted but exercised : a
freedom, not as against England, but as against all the
world.   Everywhere, but especially in countries under-
going revolutionary change, there is a tyranny of the
crowd.   When the Gaelic League decided to make
the learning of Irish compulsory, it attorned to this
tyranny.   On the other hand, Mr. Yeats, at a moment
when the Abbey Theatre seemed about to become
popular, was threatened by a fiat of this
mob-dictatorship; he was told that his theatre
must become unpopular unless he would throw
overboard most of Synge's work. By the stand which
he then made he did a greater service to freedom of the
mind in Ireland than has yet been at all recognised;
he helped to make his country fearless and strong.
Thanks mainly to him and to those who worked with
him, Ireland's thought is freer and more outspoken;
there is more thought in Ireland than there used to be.
This does not make the country easier to govern, and
just now, Ireland, if given the opportunity, would have
a hard task to govern itself.   But Ireland would
not be the only country in the world in that predica-
ment.   The schoolmaster has been abroad, and
where you have education without liberty there is

bound to be trouble. The only cure is, not to suppress education, but to give the responsibility of freedom.

I have left these papers in order as they were written, with dates annexed. One of them, *Literature among the illiterates*, was published in an earlier volume, *To-day and To-morrow in Ireland* which is now out of print. I include it here, because it completes the companion essay, called *The Life of a Song*.

My acknowledgments are due to the various publications in which they have all, except the last, previously appeared.

DUBLIN, *March*, 1919.

NOVELS OF IRISH LIFE IN THE NINETEENTH CENTURY.

"WHAT Ireland wants," said an old gentleman not very long ago, "is a Walter Scott." The remedy did not seem very practical, since Walter Scotts will not come to order, but the point of view is worth noting, for there you touch the central fact about Irish literature. We desire a Walter Scott that he may glorify our annals, popularise our legends, describe our scenery, and give an attractive view of the national character. In short, we know that Ireland possesses pre-eminently the quality of picturesqueness, and we should like to see it turned to good account. We want a Walter Scott to advertise Ireland, and to fill the hotels with tourists; but as for desiring to possess a great novelist simply for the distinction of the thing, probably no civilised people on earth is more indifferent to the matter. At present, indeed, a Walter Scott, should he appear in Ireland, would be apt to have a cold welcome. To write on anything connected with Irish history is inevitably to offend the Press of one party, and very probably of both. Lever is less of a caricaturist than Dickens, yet Dickens is idolised while Lever has been bitterly blamed for lowering Irish character in the eyes of the world; the charge is even repeated in the *Dictionary of National Biography*. That may be patriotic sentiment, but it is not criticism.

Literature in Ireland, in short, is almost inextricably connected with considerations foreign to art; it is regarded as a means, not as an end.   During the nineteenth century the belief being general among all classes of Irish people that the English know nothing of Ireland, every book on an Irish subject was judged by the effect it was likely to have upon English opinion, to which the Irish are naturally sensitive, since it decides the most important Irish questions.   But apart from this practical aspect of the matter, there is a morbid national sensitiveness which desires to be consulted.   Ireland, though she ought to count herself amply justified of her children, is still complaining that she is misunderstood among the nations; she is for ever crying out for someone to give her keener sympathy, fuller appreciation, and exhibit herself and her grievances to the world in a true light.   The result is that kind of insincerity and special pleading which has been the curse of Irish or Anglo-Irish literature.   I write of a literature which has its natural centre in Dublin, not in Connemara; which looks eastward, not westward.   That literature begins with the *Drapier Letters:* it continues through the great line of orators in whom the Irish genius (we say nothing of the Celtic) has found its highest expression; and it produced its first novelist, perhaps also its best, in the unromantic person of Maria Edgeworth.

Miss Edgeworth had a sound instinct for her art, disfigured though her later writings are by what Madame de Staël called her *triste utilité*.   Her first story is her most artistic production. *Castle Rackrent* is simply a pleasant satire upon the illiterate and improvident gentry who have always been too common

in her country. In this book she holds no brief; she
never stops to preach; her moral is implied, not
expressed. A historian might, it is true, go to *Castle
Rackrent* for information about the conditions of land
tenure as well as about social life in the Ireland of that
day; but the erudition is part and parcel of her story.
Throughout the length and breadth of Ireland, setting
aside great towns, the main interest of life for all classes
is the possession of land. Irish peasants seldom marry
for love, they never murder for love; but they marry
and they murder for land. To know something of the
land-question is indispensable for an Irish novelist, and
Miss Edgeworth graduated with honours in this
subject. She was her father's agent; when her brother
succeeded to the property she resigned, but in the
troubles of 1830 she was recalled to the management.
and saved the estate. *Castle Rackrent* is, therefore,
like Galt's *Annals of the Parish*, a historical document;
but it is none the worse story for that. The narrative
is put dramatically into the mouth of old Thady, a
lifelong servant of the family. Thady's son, Jason
Quirk, attorney and agent to the estate, has dispos-
sessed the Rackrents; but Thady is still " poor
Thady," and regards the change with horror. Before
recounting the history of his own especial master and
patron, Sir Condy Rackrent, last of the line, Thady
gives his ingenuous account of the three who previously
bore the name; Sir Patrick, Sir Murtagh, and Sir Kit.
Sir Patrick, the inventor of raspberry whiskey, died at
table : " Just as the company rose to drink his health
with three cheers, he fell down in a sort of fit, and was
carried off; they sat it out, and were surprised in the
morning to find that it was all over with poor Sir

B

Patrick." That no gentleman likes to be disturbed
after dinner, was the best recognised rule of life in
Ireland; if your host happened to have a fit, you knew
he would wish you to sit it out. Gerald Griffin in *The
Collegians* makes the same point with his usual vigour.
A shot is heard in the dining-room by the maids down-
stairs. They are for rushing in, but the manservant
knows better : " Sure, don't you know, if there was
anyone shot the master would ring the bell." After
Sir Patrick, who thus lived and died, to quote his
epitaph, " a monument of old Irish hospitality," came
Sir Murtagh, " who was a very learned man in the
law, and had the character of it "; another passion that
seems to go with the land-hunger in Ireland. Sir
Murtagh married one of the family of the Skinflints :
" She was a strict observer for self and servants of Lent
and all fast days, but not holidays." However, says
Thady (is there not a strong trace of Swift in all this?),

" However, my lady was very charitable in her own
way. She had a charity school for poor children,
where they were taught to read and write gratis, and
where they were well kept to spinning gratis for my
lady in return; for she had always heaps of duty yarn
from the tenants, and got all her household linen out
of the estate from first to last; for after the spinning,
the weavers on the estate took it in hand for nothing,
because of the looms my lady's interest could get from
the Linen Board to distribute gratis. . . . Her
table the same way, kept for next to nothing; duty
fowls, and duty turkeys, and duty geese came as fast
as we could eat them, for my lady kept a sharp look-
out and knew to a tub of butter everything the tenants
had all round. . . . As for their young pigs, we

had them, and the best bacon and hams they could make up, with all young chickens in the spring; but they were a set of poor wretches, and we had nothing but misfortunes with them, always breaking and running away. This, Sir Murtagh and my lady said, was all their former landlord, Sir Patrick's fault, who let 'em get the half year's rent into arrear; there was something in that, to be sure. But Sir Murtagh was as much the contrary way——"

I have abridged my lady's methods, and I omit Sir Murtagh's, who taught his tenants, as he said, to know the law of landlord and tenant. But, "though a learned man in the law, he was a little too incredulous in other matters." He neglected his health, broke a blood-vessel in a rage with my lady, and so made way for Sir Kit the prodigal. Sir Kit was shot in a duel, and Sir Condy came into an estate which, between Sir Murtagh's law-suits and Sir Kit's gaming, was considerably embarrassed; indeed, the story proper is simply a history of makeshifts to keep rain and bailiffs out of the family mansion. Poor Sir Condy; he was the very moral of the man who is no man's enemy but his own, and was left at the last with no friend but old Thady. Even Judy Quirk turned against him, forgetting his goodness in tossing up between her and Miss Isabella Moneygawl, the romantic lady who eloped with him after the toss. She deserted before Judy; here is a bit of the final scene. Thady was going upstairs with a slate to make up a window-pane.

" This window was in the long passage, or gallery, as my lady gave orders to have it called, in the gallery leading up to my master's bedchamber and hers. And when I went up with the slate, the door having no lock, and the bolt spoilt, was ajar after Mrs. Jane (my lady's maid), and as I was busy with the window, I heard all that was saying within. 'Well, what's in your letter, Bella, my dear?' says he. 'You're a long time spelling it over.' 'Won't you shave this morning, Sir Condy?' says she, and put the letter into her pocket. 'I shaved the day before yesterday,' says he, 'my dear, and that's not what I'm thinking of now; but anything to oblige you, and to have peace and quietness, my dear,'—and presently I had the glimpse of him at the cracked glass over the chimney-piece, standing up shaving himself to please my lady."

However, the quarrel comes on in a delightful scene, where Sir Condy shows himself at all events an amiable gentleman; and so my lady goes home to her own people. There you have Miss Edgeworth at her very best; and, indeed, *Castle Rackrent* received such a tribute as no other novel ever had paid to it. Many people have heard how when *Waverley* came to the Edgeworth household, Mr. Edgeworth, after his custom, read it aloud almost, as it would appear, at one sitting. When the end came for that fascinated circle, amid the chorus of exclamations, Mr. Edgeworth said: "What is this? *Postscript which ought to have been a preface*." Then there was a chorus of protests that he should not break the spell with prose. "Anyhow," he said, "let us hear what the man has to say," and so read on to the passage where Scott explained that he desired to do for Scotland what had been done for Ireland: "to emulate the admirable fidelity of Miss Edgeworth's portraits." What Maria

Edgeworth felt we know from the letter she posted off
" to the Author of ' Waverley,' *Aut Scotus aut
Diabolus*."

It would be unkind to compare Scott with his model.
For the poetry and the tragic power of his novels one
would never think of looking in Miss Edgeworth.   Her
work is compact of observation; yet the gifts she has
are not to be under-valued.   She is mistress of a kindly
yet searching satire, real wit, a fine vein of comedy;
and she can rise to such true pathos as dignifies the
fantastic figure of King Corny in *Ormond*, perhaps the
best thing she ever did.   But she had in her father a
literary adviser, not of the negative but of the positive
order, and there never was a more fully developed
prig than Richard Edgeworth.   His view of literature
was purely utilitarian; to convey practical lessons was
the business of all superior persons, more particularly
of an Edgeworth.   In *Castle Rackrent* his suggestions
and comments are happily relegated to the position of
notes; in the other books they form part and parcel of
the novel.   *The Absentee*, for instance, contains
admirable dialogue and many life-like figures; but the
scheme of the story conveys a sense of unreality.
Every fault or vice has its counterbalancing virtue
represented.   Lady Clonbroney, vulgarly ashamed of
her country, is set off by the patriotic Lady Oranmore;
the virtuous Mr. Burke forms too obvious a pendant to
the rascally agents old Nick and St. Dennis.   It is
needless to say that the exclusively virtuous people are
deadly dull.   It is the novel with a purpose written by
a novelist whose strength lies in the delineation of
character.   Miss Edgeworth can never carry you away
with her story, as Charles Reade sometimes can, and
make you forget and forgive the virtuous intention.

What was unreal in Miss Edgeworth became mere insincerity in her contemporary, Lady Morgan. Few people could tell you now where Thackeray got Miss Glorvina O'Dowd's baptismal name; yet *The Wild Irish Girl* had a great triumph in its day, and Glorvina stood sponsor to the milliners' and haberdashers' inventions ninety years before the apotheosis of Trilby. *O'Donnell*, which is counted Lady Morgan's best novel, gives a lively ideal portrait of the authoress, first as the governess-grub, then transformed by marriage into the butterfly-duchess. But the book is a thinly-disguised political pamphlet. "Look," she says in effect, "at the heroic virtues of O'Donnell, the young Irishman, driven to serve in foreign armies, despoiled of his paternal estates by the penal laws; look at the fidelity, the simplicity, the native humour (so dramatically effective) of his servant Rory; and then say if you will not plump for Catholic Emancipation." "My dear lady," the reader murmurs, "I wondered why you were so set upon underlining all these things. Can you not tell us a story frankly, and let us alone with your conclusions?"

Unfortunately, very much the same has to be said of a far greater writer, William Carleton, even in those tales which are based upon his own most intimate experience. *The Poor Scholar*, his most popular story, proceeds directly from an episode in his own life. He had himself been a poor scholar, had set out from his northern home to walk to Munster, where the best known schools were, trusting to charity by the way to lodge him, and to charity to keep him throughout his schooling for the sake of his vocation, and for the blessing sure to descend upon those who aided a

peasant's son to become a priest. Nothing could be
more vivid than the early scenes, the collection made
at the altar for Jimmy McEvoy, the priest's sermon,
the boy's parting from home, and the roadside hospitality; there is one infinitely touching episode in the
house of the first farmer who shelters him.. Then
come the school itself, and the tyranny of its master,
till the boy falls sick of a fever, and is turned out of
doors. Then, alas, the conventional intervenes in
the person of the virtuous absentee ignorant of his
agent's misdoings : the long arm of coincidence is
stretched to the uttermost; and we have to wade
through pages of discussion upon the relations of landlord and tenant till we are put wholly out of tune for
the beautiful scene of Jimmy's return home in his
priestly dress.

Carleton did for the peasantry what Miss Edgeworth
had done for the upper classes. In her books the
peasants have only an incidental part, and she
describes them shrewdly and sympathetically enough,
but with a mind untouched either by their faith or by
their superstitions; seeing their good and bad qualities
clearly in a dry light, but never in imagination identify-
ing herself with them. Superior to Miss Edgeworth
in power and insight, he is immeasurably her inferior
in literary skill. One should remember, in comment-
ing upon the poverty of Irish literature in English,
that, so far as concerns imaginative work, it began in
the nineteenth century. Carleton only died in 1869,
Miss Edgeworth in 1849; and before them there is no
one.

On the other hand the speech of Lowland Scots, with
whose richness in masterpieces our poverty is naturally

contrasted, has been employed for literature as long as the vernacular English.   A king of Scotland wrote admirable verse in the generation after Chaucer; the influence of the Court fostered poetry, and the close intercourse with France kept Scotch writers in touch with first-rate models.   Dunbar, strolling as a friar in France, may have known Villon, whom he often resembles.   In Ireland, till a century ago, English was as much a foreign language as Norman French in England under the Plantagenets.   Among the English Protestants, settled in Ireland, and separated by a hard line of cleavage from the Catholic population, there arose great men in letters, Goldsmith, Burke, Sheridan, who showed their Irish temperament in their handling of English themes.   But in Ireland itself, before the events of 1782 added importance to Dublin, there was no centre for a literature to gather round.   Such national pride as exists in English-speaking Ireland dates from the days of Grattan and Flood.   And Irish national aspirations still bear the impress of their origin amid that period of political turmoil, than which nothing is more hostile to the brooding care of literary workmanship, the long labour and the slow result.   Irishmen have always shown a strong disinclination to pure literature.   The roll of Irish novelists is more than half made up of women's names; Miss Edgeworth, Lady Morgan, Miss Emily Lawless, and Miss Jane Barlow.   Journalists Ireland has produced as copiously as orators; the writers of The Spirit of the Nation, that admirable collection of stirring poems, are journalists working in verse; and Carleton, falling under their influence, became a journalist working in fiction.   In his pages, even when the debater ceases to argue and harangue, the style is still journalistic, except in those passages where his dramatic instinct puts living speech into the mouths of men and women. Politics so monopolise the minds of Irishmen, newspapers so make up their whole reading, that the class to which Carleton and the poet Mangan belonged have never fully entered upon the heritage of English literature. If an English peasant knows nothing else, he knows the Bible and very likely Bunyan; but a Roman Catholic population has little commerce with that pure fountain of style. Genius cannot dispense with models, and Carleton and Mangan had the worst possible. Yet when it has been said that Carleton was a half-educated peasant, writing in a language whose best literature he had not sufficiently assimilated to feel the true value of words, it remains to be said that he was a great novelist. He cannot be fairly illustrated by quotation; but read any of his stories and see if he does not bring up vividly before you Ireland as it was before the famine; Ireland still swarming with beggars who marched about in families subsisting chiefly on the charity of the poor; Ireland of which the hedge-school was plainly to him the most characteristic institution.

Carleton does not stand by himself; he is the head and representative of a whole class of Irish novelists, among whom John Banim is the best known name. All of them were peasants who aimed at depicting scenes of peasant life from their own experience. What one may call the melodramatic Irish story, in which Lever was so brilliantly successful, has its first famous example in *The Collegians* of Gerald Griffin. The novel has no concern with college life, and is far

better described by its stage-title, *The Colleen Bawn.*
Here at least is a man with a story to tell and no object
but to tell it. Griffin belonged to the lay order of
Christian Brothers : his book deals principally with a
society no more familiar to him than was the household
of Mr. Rochester to Charlotte Brontë; and his method
recalls the Brontës by its strenuous imagination and its
vehement painting of passion. The tale was suggested
by a murder which excited all Ireland. A young
southern squire carried off a girl with some money,
and procured her death by drowning. He was arrested
at his mother's house and a terrible scene took place,
terribly rendered in the book. Griffin, of course,
changes the motive; the girl is carried off not for money
but for love, and she is sacrificed to make way for a
stronger passion. Eily O'Connor, the victim, is a
pretty and pathetic figure; the hero-villain Hardress
Cregan, and the mother who indirectly causes the
crime, are effective though melodramatic; but the
actual murderer, Danny the Lord, Hardress Cregan's
familiar, is worthy of Scott or Hugo.

In his sketches of society, Hyland Creagh, the duel-
list, old Cregan, and the rest, Griffin is describing a
state of affairs previous to his own experience, the
Ireland of Sir Jonah Barrington's memoirs; he is not,
as were Carleton and Miss Edgeworth, copying min-
utely from personal observation. Herein he resembles
Lever who, when all is said and done, remains the
chief, as he is the most Irish, of Irish novelists. It is
true that Lever had two distinct manners; and in his
later books he deals chiefly with contemporary society,
drawing largely on his experiences of diplomatic life.

Like most novelists he preferred his later work; but
the books by which he is best known, *Harry Lorrequer*
and the rest, are his earliest productions; and though
his maturer skill was employed on different subjects,
he formed his imagination in studies of the Napoleonic
Wars and of a duelling, drinking, bailiff-beating
Ireland. His point of view never altered, and the
peculiar attraction of his writings is always the same.
Lever's books have the quality rather of speech than
of writing; wherever you open the pages there is
always a witty, well-informed Irishman discoursing to
you, who tells his story admirably, when he has one to
tell, and, failing that, never fails to be pleasant. Irish
talk is apt to be discursive; to rely upon a general
charm diffused through the whole, rather than upon
any quotable brilliancy; its very essence is spontaneity,
high spirits, fertility of resource. That is a fair
description of Lever. He is never at a loss. If his
story hangs, off he goes at score with a perfectly irrele-
vant anecdote, but told with such enjoyment of the
joke that you cannot resent the digression. Indeed the
plots are left pretty much to take care of themselves;
he positively preferred to write his stories in monthly
instalments for a magazine; he is not a conscientious
artist, but he lays himself out to amuse you, and he
does it. If he advertises a character as a wit, he does
not labour phrases to describe his brilliancy; he pro-
duces the witticisms. He has been accused of exag-
geration. As regards the incidents, one can only say
that the memoirs of Irish society at the beginning of
this century furnish at least fair warranty for any of his
inventions. In character-drawing he certainly overcharged the traits; but he did so with intention, and by

consistently heightening the tones throughout obtained an artistic impression, which had life behind it, however ingeniously travestied. His stories have no unity of action, but through a great diversity of characters and incidents they maintain their unity of treatment. That is not the highest ideal of the novel, but it is an intelligible one, not lacking famous examples; and Lever perfectly understood it.

If one wishes to realise how good an artist Lever was, the best way is to read his contemporary Samuel Lover. *Handy Andy* appeared somewhat later than *Harry Lorrequer*. It is just the difference between good whiskey and bad whiskey; both are indigenous and therefore characteristic, but let us be judged by our best. Obviously the men have certain things in common; great natural vivacity, and an easy cheerful way of looking at life. Lover can raise a laugh, but his wit is horseplay except for a few happy phrases. He has no real comedy; there is nothing in *Handy Andy* half so ingenious as the story in *Jack Hinton* of the way Ulick Bourke acquitted himself of his debt to Father Tom. And behind all Lever's conventional types there is a real fund of observation and knowledge which is absolutely wanting in Lover, who simply lacked the brains to be anything more than a trifler.

A very different talent was that of their younger contemporary J. Sheridan Le Fanu. The author of *Uncle Silas* had plenty of solid power; but his art was too highly specialised. No one ever succeeded better in two main objects of the story-teller; first, in exciting interest, in stimulating curiosity by vague hints of some dreadful mystery; and then in concentrating attention upon a dramatic scene. It is true that, although an

Irishman, he gained his chief successes with stories
that had an English setting; but one of the best, *The
House by the Churchyard*, describes very vividly life
at Chapelizod in the days when this deserted little
village, which lies just beyond the Phœnix Park, was
thickly peopled with the families of officers stationed
in Dublin. Yet somehow one does not carry away
from the reading of it any picture of that society; the
story is so exciting that the mind has no time to rest
on details, but hurries on from clue to clue till finally
and literally the murder is out. Books which keep a
reader on the tenter-hooks of conjecture must always
suffer from this undue concentration of the interest;
and in spite of cheery, inquisitive Dr. Toole, and the
remarkable sketch of Black Dillon, the ruffianly genius
with a reputation only recognised in the hospitals and
the police-courts (a character admirably invented and
admirably used in the plot) one can hardly class Le
Fanu among those novelists who have left memorable
presentments of Irish life. It is a pity; for plainly, if
the man had cared less for sensational incident and
ingenious construction, he might have sketched life
and character with a strong brush and a kind of grim
realism.

Realism Lever does not aim at; he declines to be on
his oath about anything. What he gives one, vividly
enough, is national colour, not local colour; he is essentially Irish, just as Fielding is essentially English; but
he aims at verisimilitude rather than veracity. The
ideal of the novel has changed since his day. Compare him with the two ladies who stand out promi-
nently among contemporary writers of Irish fiction,
Miss Jane Barlow and Miss Emily Lawless. To begin

with, Lever's stories are always concerned with the
Quality; peasants only come in for an underplot, or in
subordinate parts; and the gentry all through Ireland
resemble one another within reasonable limits.   It is
different with the peasantry.   In every part of Ireland
you will find people who have never been ten miles
away from the place of their birth, and upon whom a
local character is unmistakably stamped.   The contemporary novelists delight to mark these differences,
these salient points of singularity; and their studies are
chiefly of the peasantry.   They settle down upon some
little corner of the country and never stir out of it.
Miss Lawless is not content to get you Irish character;
she must show you a Clare man or an Arran islander,
and she is at infinite pains to point out how his nature,
even his particular actions, are influenced by the place
of his bringing up.   Lever avoids this specialisation;
he prefers a stone wall country for his hunting scenes,
but beyond that he goes no further into details.   Again
Miss Lawless both in *Grania* and in *Hurrish* makes
you aware that young Irishmen of Hurrish's class are
curiously indifferent to female beauty.   Lever will
have none of that; his Irishman must be " a divil with
the girls," although Lever is no sentimentalist, and does
not talk of love matches among the Irish peasantry.

The greatest divergence of all, however, is in the
temper attributed to the Irish.   Lever makes them gay,
Miss Lawless and Miss Barlow make them sad.   No
one denies that sadness is nearer the reality, but it is
unreasonable to call Lever insincere.   Naturally careless and lighthearted he does not trouble himself with
the riddle of the painful world; the distress which
touches him most nearly is a distress for debt.   But if

Lever is not realistic he is natural; he follows the law
of his nature as an artist should; he sees life through
his own medium; and if books are to be valued as
companions, not many of them are better company
than *Charles O'Malley* or *Lord Kilgobbin*; for first and
last Lever was always himself.

Yet, I must own it, it does not do to read Lever soon
after Miss Barlow. Her stories of Lisconnel and its
folk have a tragic dignity wholly out of his range. It
is a sad-coloured country she writes of, gray and
brown; sodden brown with bog water, gray with rock
cropping up through the fields; the only brightness is
up overhead in the heavens, and even they are often
clouded. These sombre hues, with the passing gleam
of something above them, reflect themselves in every
page of her books. She renders that complete harmony between the people and their surroundings which
is only seen in working folk whose clothes are stained
with the colour of the soil they live by, and whose
lives assimilate themselves to its character. She has
a fineness of touch, a poetry, to which no other Irish
story-teller has attained.

Yet, Miss Barlow has never succeeded with a regular novel: and she may have been only a forerunner.
All great writers proceed from a school, and there does
exist now undeniably a school of Irish literature which
differs from Miss Edgeworth in being strongly tinged
with the element of Celtic romance, from Carleton in
possessing an admirable standard of style, and from
Lever in aiming at a sincere and vital portraiture of
Irish life.

1897.

A CENTURY OF IRISH HUMOUR.

N a preface to the French translation of Sienkiewicz's works, M. de Wyzewa, the well-known critic, himself a Pole, makes a suggestive comparison between the Polish and the Russian natures. The Pole, he says, is quicker, wittier, more imaginative, more studious of beauty, less absorbed in the material world than the Russian—in a word, infinitely more gifted with the artistic temperament; and yet in every art the Russian has immeasurably outstripped the Pole. His explanation, if not wholly convincing, is at least suggestive. The Poles are a race of dreamers, and the dreamer finds his reward in himself. He does not seek to conquer the world with arms or with commerce, with tears or with laughter; neither money tempts him nor fame, and the strenuous, unremitting application which success demands, whether in war, business, or the arts, is alien to his being.

The same observation and the same reasoning apply with equal force to the English and the Irish. No one who has lived in the two countries will deny that the Irish are apparently the more gifted race; no one can deny, if he has knowledge and candour, that the English have accomplished a great deal more, the Irish a great deal less. Nowhere is this more evident than in the productions of that faculty which Irishmen have always been reputed, and justly reputed, to possess in peculiar measure—the faculty of humour.

Compare Lever, who for a long time passed as the typical Irish humorist, with his contemporaries Thackeray and Dickens. The comparison is not fair, but it suggests the central fact that the humour of Irish literature is deficient in depth, in intellectual quality, or, to put it after an Irish fashion, in gravity.

'Humorous' is a word as question-begging as 'artistic,' and he would be a rash man who should try to define either. But so much as this will readily be admitted, that humour is a habit of mind essentially complex, involving always a double vision—a reference from the public or normal standard of proportion to one that is private and personal. The humorist refuses to part with any atom of his own personality, he stamps it on whatever comes from him. "If reasons were as plenty as blackberries," says Falstaff, achieving individuality by the same kind of odd picturesque comparison as every witty Irish peasant uses in talk, to the delight of himself and his hearers. But the individuality lies deeper than phrases; Falstaff takes his private standard into battle with him. There is nothing more obviously funny than the short paunchy man, let us not say cowardly, but disinclined to action, who finds himself engaged in a fight. Lever has used him a score of times (beginning with Mr. O'Leary in the row at a gambling-hell in Paris), and whether he runs or whether he fights, his efforts to do either are grotesquely laughable. Shakespeare puts that view of Falstaff too: Prince Hal words it. But Falstaff, the humorist in person, rises on the field of battle over the slain Percy and enunciates his philosophy of the better part of valour. Falstaff's estimate of honour—" that word honour " "' Who hath it? he that died o' Wed-

c

nesday   Doth he feel it?''), the "grinning honour" that Sir Walter Blunt wears where the Douglas left him—is necessary to complete the humorist's vision of a battle-piece.   Lever will scarcely visit you with such reflections, for the humorist of Lever's type never stands stands apart and smiles; he laughs loud and in company.   Still less will he give you one of those speeches which are the supreme achievement of this faculty, where the speaker's philosophy is not reasoned out liked Falstaff's, but revealed in a flash of the onlooker's insight.   Is it pardonable to quote the account of Falstaff's death as the hostess narrates it?

"How now, Sir John, quoth I, what, man! be of good cheer. So a' cried out God, God, three or four times.   Now I, to comfort him, bid him a' should not think of God; I hoped there was no need to trouble himself with any such thoughts yet."

Humour can go no farther than that terrible, illuminating phrase, which is laughable enough, heaven knows, but scarce likely to make you laugh.   Contrast the humour of that with the humour of such a story as Lever delighted in.   There were two priests dining with a regiment, we all have read in *Harry Lorrequer*, who chaffed a dour Ulster Protestant till he was the open derision of the mess.   Next time they returned, the Protestant major was radiant with a geniality that they could not explain till they had to make their way out of barracks in a hurry, and found that the countersign (arranged by the major) was "Bloody end to the Pope."   Told as Lever tells it, with all manner of jovial amplifications, that story would make anyone laugh.   But it does not go deep.   The thing is funny in too obvious a way; the mirth finds too large an

outlet in laughter; it does not hang about the brain,
inextricable from the processes of thought; it carries
nothing with it beyond the jest.   And just as tears
help to an assuaging of grief, so in a sense laughter
makes an end of mirth.   Give a feeling its instinctive
vent, and you will soon be done with it, like the child
who laughs and cries within five minutes; check it,
and it spreads inward, gaining in intellectual quality
as it loses in physical expression.   The moral is, that
if you wish to be really humorous you must not be too
funny; and the capital defect of most Irish humour is
that its aim is too simple—it does not look beyond
raising a laugh.

There are brilliant exceptions in the century that
lies between Sheridan and Mr. Bernard Shaw, between
Maria Edgeworth and Miss Barlow.   But serious art
or serious thought in Ireland has always revealed itself
to the English sooner or later as a species of sedition,
and the Irish have with culpable folly allowed themselves to accept for characteristic excellences what
were really the damning defects of their work—an easy
fluency of wit, a careless spontaneity of laughter.   They
have taken Moore for a great poet, and Handy Andy
for a humorist to be proud of.   Yet an Irishman who
wishes to speak dispassionately must find humour of a
very different kind from that of *Handy Andy* or *Harry
Lorrequer* either, to commend without reserve, as a
thing that may be put forward to rank with what is
best in other literatures.

Taking Sheridan and Miss Edgeworth as marking
the point of departure, it becomes obvious that one is
at an end, the other at a beginning.   Sheridan belongs
body and soul to the eighteenth century; Miss Edge-

worth, though her name sounds oddly in that context, is part and parcel of the romantic movement. The " postscript which ought to have been a preface " to *Waverley* declared, though after Scott's magnificent fashion, a real indebtedness. Sheridan's humour, essentially metropolitan, had found no use for local colour; Miss Edgeworth before Scott proved the artistic value that could be extracted from the characteristics of a special breed of people under special circumstances in a special place. Mr. Yeats, who, like all poets, is a most suggestive and a most misleading critic, has declared that modern Irish literature begins with Carleton. That is only true if we are determined to look in Irish literature for qualities that can be called Celtic—if we insist that the outlook on the world shall be the Catholic's or the peasant's. Miss Edgeworth had not a trace of the Celt—as I conceive that rather indefinite entity—about her; but she was as good an Irishwoman as ever walked, and there are hundreds of Irish people of her class and creed looking at Irish life with kindly humorous Irish eyes, seeing pretty much what she saw, enjoying it as she enjoyed it, but with neither her power nor her will to set it down. *Castle Rackrent* is a masterpiece; and had Miss Edgeworth been constant to the dramatic method which she then struck out for herself, with all the fine reticences that it involved, her name might have stood high in literature. Unhappily, her too exemplary father repressed the artist in her, fostered the pedagogue, and in her later books she commits herself to an attitude in which she can moralise explicitly upon the ethical and social bearings of every word and action. The fine humour in *Ormond* is obscured by its setting; in *Castle*

Rackrent the humour shines.   Sir Condy and his lady we see none the less distinctly for seeing them through the eyes of old Thady, the retainer who narrates the Rackrent history; and in the process we have a vision of old Thady himself.   Now and then the novelist reminds us of her presence by some extravagantly ironic touch, as when Thady describes Sir Condy's anger with the Government " about a place that was promised him and never given, after his supporting them against his conscience very honourably and being greatly abused for, he having the name of a great patriot in the country."   Thady would hardly have been so ingenuous as that.   But for the most part the humour is truly inherent in the situation, and you might look far for a better passage than the description of Sir Condy's parting with his lady.   But it is better to illustrate from a scene perhaps less genuinely humorous, but more professedly so—Sir Condy's wake.   Miss Edgeworth does not dwell on the broad farce of the entertainment; she does not make Thady eloquent over the whisky that was drunk and the fighting that began and so forth, as Lever or Carleton would certainly have been inclined to do. She fixes on the central comedy of the situation, Sir Condy's innocent vanity and its pitiable disappointment—is it necessary to recall that he had arranged for the wake himself, because he always wanted to see his own funeral?   Poor Sir Condy!—even Thady, who was in the secret, had forgotten all about him, when he was startled by the sound of his master's voice from under the greatcoats thrown all atop.

"'Thady,' says he, 'I've had enough of this; I'm smothering and can't hear a word of all they're saying of the deceased.' 'God bless you, and lie still and quiet a bit longer,' says I, ' for my sister's afraid of ghosts, and would die on the spot with fright if she was to see you come to life all on a sudden this way without the least preparation.'   So he lays him still, though well-nigh stifled, and I made haste to tell the secret of the joke, whispering to one and t'other, and there was a great surprise, but not so great as he had laid out there would.   ' And aren't we to have the pipes and tobacco after coming so far to-night?' said some one; but they were all well enough pleased when his honour got up to drink with them, and sent for more spirits from a shebeen house where they very civilly let him have it upon credit.   So the night passed off very merrily; but to my mind Sir Condy was rather upon the sad order in the midst of it all, not finding there had been such great talk about himself after his death as that he had always expected to hear.''

In the end Sir Condy died, not by special arrangement. "He had but a poor funeral after all," is Thady's remark; and you see with the kindly double vision of the humorist Thady's sincere regret for the circumstance that would most have afflicted the deceased, as well as the more obviously comic side of Thady's comment and Sir Condy's lifelong aspiration. Indeed, the whole narrative is shot with many meanings, and one never turns to it without a renewed faculty of laughter.

If it were necessary to compare true humour with the make-believe, a comparison might be drawn between Thady and the servant in Lady Morgan's novel *O'Donnell*. Rory is the stage Irishman in all his commonest attitudes. But it is better to go straight on, and concern ourselves solely with the work of real literary quality, and Carleton falls next to be considered.

Of genius with inadequate equipment it is always difficult to speak. Carleton is the nearest thing to Burns that we have to show; and his faults, almost

insuperable to the ordinary reader, are the faults
which Burns seldom failed to display when writing in
English. But to Burns there was given an instrument
perfected by long centuries of use—the Scotch vernacular song and ballad; Carleton had to make his
own, and the genius for form was lacking in him.
Some day there may come a man of pure Irish race
who will be to Carleton what Burns was to Ferguson,
and then Ireland will have what it lacks; moreover, in
the light of his achievement we shall see better what
the pioneer accomplished. Every gift that Carleton
had—and pathos and humour, things complementary
to each other, he possessed in profusion—every gift
is obscured by faulty technique. Nearly every trait is
overcharged; for instance, in his story of the *Midnight
Mass* he rings the changes interminably upon the old
business of the wonderful medicine in the vagrants'
blessed horn that had a strong odour of whisky; but
what an admirably humorous figure is this same
Darby O'More! Out of the *Poor Scholar* alone, that
inchoate masterpiece, you could illustrate a dozen
phases of Carleton's mirth, beginning with the famous
sermon where the priest so artfully wheedles and
coaxes his congregation into generosity towards the
boy who is going out on the world, and all the while
unconsciously displays his own laughable and lovable
weaknesses. There you have the double vision, that
helps to laugh with the priest, and to laugh at him in
the same breath, as unmistakably as in the strange
scene of the famine days where the party of mowers
find Jimmy sick of the fever by the wayside and
"schame a day" from their employer to build him a
rough shelter. That whole chapter, describing the

indefatigable industry with which they labour on the
voluntary task, their glee in the truantry from the
labour for which they are paid, their casuistry over
the theft of milk for the pious puprose of keeping the
poor lad alive, the odd blending of cowardice and
magnanimity in their terror of the sickness and in
their constant care that some one should at least be
always in earshot of the boy, ready to pass in to him
on a long-handed shovel what food they could scrape
up, their supple ingenuity in deceiving the pompous
landlord who comes to oversee their work,—all that
is the completest study in existence of Irish character
as it came to be under the system of absolute dependence.   There is nothing so just as true humour, for
by the law of its being it sees inevitably two sides;
and this strange compound of vices and virtues, so
rich in all the softer qualities, so lacking in all the
harder ones, stands there in Carleton's pages, neither
condemned nor justified, but seen and understood
with a kindly insight.   Carleton is the document of
documents for Ireland in the years before the famine,
preserving a record of conditions material and spiritual, which happily have largely ceased to exist, yet
operate indefinitely as causes among us, producing
eternal though eternally modifiable effects.

But, for the things in human nature that are neither
of yesterday, to-day, nor to-morrow, but unchange-
able, he has the humorist's true touch.   When the
poor scholar is departing, and has actually torn himself away from home, his mother runs after him with
a last token—a small bottle of holy water. " Jimmy,
alanna," said she, " here's this an' carry it about you
—it will keep evil from you; an' be sure to take good

care of the written characther you got from the priest
an' Squire Benson; an', darlin', don't be lookin' too
often at the cuff o' your coat, for feard the people
might get a notion that you have the banknotes sewed
in it. An', Jimmy agra, don't be too lavish upon
their Munsther crame; they say 'tis apt to give people
the ague. Kiss me agin, agra, an' the heavens above
keep you safe and well till we see you once more."

Through all that catalogue of precautions, divine
and human, one feels the mood between tears and
laughter of the man who set it down. But I think you
only come to the truth about Carleton in the last scene
of all, when Jimmy returns to his home, a priest.
Nothing could be more stilted, more laboured, than
the pages which attempt to render his emotions and
his words, till there comes the revealing touch. His
mother at sight of him, returned unlooked-for after the
long absence, loses for a moment the possession of her
faculties, and cannot be restored. At last, " I will
speak to her," said Jimmy, " in Irish; it will go
directly to her heart." And it does.

Carleton never could speak to us in Irish; the English was still a strange tongue on his lips and in the
ears of those he lived among; and his work comes
down distracted between the two languages, imper-
fect and halting, only with flashes of true and living
speech.

When you come to Lever, it is a very different
story. Lever was at no lack for utterance; nobody
was ever more voluble, no one ever less inclined to
sit and bite his pen, waiting for the one and only word.
Good or bad, he could be trusted to rattle on; and, as
Trollope said, if you pulled him out of bed and

demanded something witty, he would flash it at you
before he was half awake. Some people are born
with the perilous gift of improvisation; and the best
that can be said for Lever is that he is the nearest equivalent in Irish literature, or in English either, to the
marvellous faculty of D'Artagnan's creator. He has
the same exuberance, the same inexhaustible supply
of animal spirits, of invention that is always spirited,
of wit that goes off like fireworks. He delighted a
whole generation of readers, and one reader at least
in this generation he still delights; but I own that to
enjoy him you must have mastered the art of skip-
ping. Whether you take him in his earlier manner,
in the " Charles O'Malley " vein of adventure, fox-
hunting, steeple-chasing, Peninsular fighting, or in
his later more intellectual studies of shady financiers,
needy political adventurers, and the whole generation
of usurers and blacklegs, he is always good; but alas
and alas, he is never good enough. His work is
rotten with the disease of anecdote; instead of that
laborious concentration on a single character ·which
is necessary for any kind of creative work, but above
all for humorous creation, he presents you with a
sketch, a passing glimpse, and when you look to see
the suggestion followed out he is off at score with a
story. In the first chapter of *Davenport Dunn*, for
instance, there is an Irish gentleman on the Conti-
nent, a pork-butcher making his first experience of
Italy, hit off to the life. But a silhouette—and a very
funny silhouette—is all that we get of Mr. O'Reilly,
and the figures over whom Lever had taken trouble—
for in that work Lever did take trouble—are not seen
with humour. Directly he began to think, his

humour left him; it is as if he had been funny in watertight compartments. And perhaps that is why, here as elsewhere, he shrank from the necessary concentration of thought.

There is always a temptation to hold a brief for Lever, because he has been most unjustly censured by Irishmen, even in so august and impartial a court as the *Dictionary of National Biography*, as if he had traduced his countrymen. Did Thackeray, then, malign the English? The only charge that may fairly be brought against him is the one that cannot be rebutted—the charge of superficiality and of scamped work, of a humour that only plays over the surface of things—a humour which sees only the comic side that anybody might see. And because I cannot defend him, I say no more. Lever is certainly not a great humorist, but he is delightful company.

One may mention in passing the excursions into broad comedy of another brilliant Irishman—Le Fanu's short stories in the *Purcell Papers*, such as the *Quare Gander*, or *Billy Molowney's Taste of Love and Glory*. These are good examples of a particular literary type—the humorous anecdote—in which Irish humour has always been fertile, and of which the *ne plus ultra* is Sir Samuel Ferguson's magnificent squib in Blackwood, *Father Tom and the Pope*. Everybody knows the merits of that story, its inexhaustible fertility of comparison, its dialectic ingenuity, its jovialty, its drollery, its Rabelaisian laughter. But, after all, the highest type of humour is humour applying itself to the facts of life, and this is burlesque humour squandering itself in riot upon a delectable fiction. Humour is a great deal more than a plaything; it is a force, a weapon—at once sword and shield. If there is to be an art of literature in Ireland that can be called national, it cannot afford to devote humour solely to the production of trifles. *Father Tom* is a trifle, a splendid toy; and what is more, a trifle wrought in a moment of ease by perhaps the most serious and conscientious artist that ever made a contribution to the small body of real Irish literature in the tongue that is now native to the majority of Irishmen.

Of contemporaries, with one exception, I do not propose to speak at any length, nor can I hope that my review will be complete. There is first and foremost Miss Barlow, a lady whose work is so gentle, so unassuming, that one hears little of it in the rush and flare of these strident times, but who will be heard and listened to with fresh emotion as the stream is heard when the scream and rattle of a railway train have passed away into silence. Is she a humorist? Not in the sense of provoking laughter—and yet the things that she sees and loves and dwells on would be unbearable if they were not seen through a delicate mist of mirth. The daily life of people at continual handgrips with starvation, their little points of honour, their little questions of precedence, the infinite generosity that concerns itself with the expenditure of sixpence, the odd shifts they resort to that a gift may not have the appearance of charity,—all these are set down with a tenderness of laughter that is peculiarly and distinctively Irish.

Yet, though we may find a finer quality of humour in those writers who do not seek to raise a laugh—for instance, the subtle pervasive humour in Mr. Yeats's

Celtic Twilight—still there are few greater attractions
than that of open healthy laughter of the contagious
sort ; and it would be black ingratitude not to pay tribute to the authoresses of *Some Experiences of an
Irish R.M.*—a book that no decorous person can read
with comfort in a railway carriage.   These ladies
have the keenest eye for the obvious humours of Irish
life, they have abundance of animal spirits, and they
have that knack at fluent description embroidered with
a wealth of picturesque details that is shared by hundreds of peasants in Ireland, but is very rare indeed
on the printed page. And, mingling with the broad
farce there is a deal of excellent comedy—for instance,
in the person of old Mrs. Knox of Aussolas.   But
there is the same point to insist on—and since these
witty and delightful ladies have already the applause
of all the world one insists less unwillingly—this kind
of thing, admirable as it is, will not redeem Irish
humour from the reproach of trifling.   But in the
novel, *The Real Charlotte*, there is humour as grim
almost as Swift's—and as completely un-English ; it is
a humour which assuredly stirs more faculties than
the simple one of laughter.

   There is indeed a literature which, if not always
exactly humorous, is closely allied to it—the literature
of satire and invective ; and in this Ireland has always
been prolific. In the days of the old kings the order of
bards had grown so numerous, that they comprised a
third of the whole population, and they devoted themselves with such talent and zeal to the task of invective that no man could live in peace, and the country
cried out against them, and there was talk of suppress-
ing the whole order.   The king spared them on con-

dition that they would mend their manners.   We
have those bards still, but nowadays we call them
politicians and journalists; and frankly I think we are
ripe for another intervention, if only in the interests of
literature.   So much good talent goes to waste in bad
words; and, moreover, an observance of the decencies
is always salutary for style.   And it seems that as the
years have gone on, humour has diminished in Irish
politics, while bad humour has increased; and therefore I leave alone any attempt to survey the humour
of the orators, though Curran tempts one at the beginning and Mr. Healy at the close.   Of purely literary
satire there has been little enough, apart from its
emergence in the novel; but there is one example
which deserves to be recalled.   I have never professed
enthusiasm for Thomas Moore, but I am far indeed
from agreeing with a recent critic who would claim
literary rank for him rather in virtue of the *Fudge
Family* than of the Irish Melodies.   That satire does
not seem to get beyond brilliancy; it is very clever,
and not much more.   Still, there are passages in it
which cannot be read without enjoyment; and one
quotation may be permitted, since it puts with perfect
distinctness what it is always permissible to put—the
English case against Ireland.

> I'm a plain man who speak the truth,
>   And trust you'll think me not uncivil
> When I declare that from my youth
>   I've wished your country at the devil.
> Nor can I doubt indeed from all
>   I've heard of your high patriot fame,
> From every word your lips let fall,
>   That you most truly wish the same.

It plagues one's life out; thirty years
Have I had dinning in my ears—
Ireland wants this and that and t'other;
   And to this hour one nothing hears
But the same vile eternal bother.
   While of those countless things she wanted,
Thank God, but little has been granted.

The list of writers of humorous verse in Ireland is a
long one, but a catalogue of ephemera.   Even Father
Prout at this time of day is little more than a dried
specimen labelled for reference, or at most preserved
in vitality by the immortal *Groves of Blarney*.   But
neither that work, nor even *The Night before Larry
was stretched*, nor Le Fanu's ballad of *Shemus
O'Brien*, can rank altogether as literature.   About the
humorous song I need only say that, so far as my
experience goes, there is one, and one only, which a
person with no taste for music and some taste for
literature can hear frequently with pleasure, and that
song of course is *Father O'Flynn*.   To recall the
delightful ingenuity and the nimble wit shown by
another Irishman of the same family in the *Hawarden
Horace*, and in a lesser degree by Mr. Godley in his
Musa Frivola, leads naturally to the inquiry why
humour from Aristophanes to Carlyle has always preferred the side of reaction—a question that would
need an essay, or a volume, all to itself.

But the central question is after all why in a race
where humour is so preponderant in the racial temperament does so little of the element crystallise itself
in literature.   Humour ranks with the water power as
one of the great undeveloped resources of the country.
Something indeed has been done in the past with the
river of laughter that almost every Irish person has

flowing in his heart; but infinitely more might be done
if these rivers were put in harness.

Yet, take away two Irish names from the field of
modern comedy in the English language written during the nineteenth century, and you have uncommonly
little for which literary merit can be claimed.   The
quality of Oscar Wilde's is scarcely disputed.   There
is the more reason to dwell on Mr. Bernard Shaw's
plays, because they have not even in the twentieth
century been fully accepted by that queer folk, the
theatre-going public.   But I never yet heard of anyone who saw *You Never can Tell,* and was not amused
by it.   That was a farce, no doubt, but a farce which
appealed to emotions less elementary than those which
are touched by the spectacle of a man sitting down by
accident on his hat; it was a farce of intellectual
absurdities, of grotesque situations arising out of per-
versities of character and opinion; a farce that you
could laugh at without a loss of self-respect.   But it is
rather by his comedies than by his farces that Mr.
Shaw should be judged.   If they are not popular, it is
for a very good reason : Mr. Shaw's humour is too
serious.   His humour is a strong solvent, and one of
the many things about which this humorist is in deadly
earnest is the fetish worship of tradition.   To that he
persists in applying—in *Candida* as in half a dozen
other plays—the ordeal by laughter—an ordeal which
every human institution is bound to face.   *Candida*
will not only make people laugh, it will make them
think; and it is not easy to induce the public to think
after dinner on unaccustomed lines.   They will laugh
when they have been used to laugh, weep when they
have been used to weep; but if you ask them to laugh

when they expect to weep, or *vice versâ*, the public
will resent the proceeding.   The original humorist,
like every other original artist, has got slowly and
laboriously to convert his public before he can con-
vince them of his right to find tears and laughter
where he can.

Whatever Mr. Shaw touches, whether it be the half-
hysterical impulse that sometimes passes current for
heroism, as in *Arms and the Man*, or, as in the *Devil's
Disciple*, the conventional picturesqueness of a Don
Juan—that maker of laws, breaker of hearts, so familiar with the limelight, so unused to the illumination
by laughter, who finds himself in the long run deplor-
ably stigmatised as a saint—there is a flood of light
let in upon all manner of traditional poses, literary
insincerities that have crept into life.   There are few
things of more value in a commonwealth than such a
searching faculty of laughter.   Like Sheridan, Mr.
Shaw lives in England, and uses his comic gift for the
most part on subjects suggested to him by English
conditions of life, but with a strength of intellectual
purpose that Sheridan never possessed.   Irishmen
may wish that he found his material in Ireland.   But
an artist must take what his hand finds, and there is
no work in the world more full of the Scottish spirit or
the Scottish humour than Carlyle's *French Revolution*.
If it be asked whether Mr. Shaw's humour is typically
Irish, I must reply by another question : " Could his
plays have conceivably been written by any but an
Irishman ?"

Is there, in fact, a distinctively Irish humour ?   In a
sense, yes, no doubt, just as the English humour is of
a different quality from the Greek or the French.   But

D

nobody wants to pin down English humour to the formula of a definition; no one wants to say, Thus far shalt thou go, and beyond that shalt cease to be English. Moreover, a leading characteristic of the Irish type is just its variety—its continual deviation from the normal. How, then, to find a description that will apply to a certain quality of mind throughout a variable race; that quality being in its essence the most complete expression of an individuality, in its difference from other individualities, since a man's humour is the most individual thing about him? Description is perhaps more possible than definition. One may say that the Irish humour is kindly and lavish; that it tends to express itself in an exuberance of phrase, a wild riot of comparisons; that it amplifies rather than retrenches, finding its effects by an accumulation of traits, and not by a concentration. The vernacular Irish literature is there to prove that Irish fancy gives too much rather than too little One may observe, again, that a nation laughs habitually over its besetting weakness; and if the French find their mirth by preference in dubious adventures, it cannot be denied that much Irish humour has a pronounced alcoholic flavour. But it is better neither to define nor to describe; there is more harmful misunderstanding caused by setting down this or that quality, this or that person, as typically French, typically English, typically Irish, than by any other fallacy; and we Irish have suffered peculiarly by the notion that the typical Irishman is the funny man of the empire. What I would permit myself to assert is, first, that the truest humour is not just the light mirth that comes easily from the lips—that, in the hackneyed phrase, bubbles over spontaneously—but is the expression of deep feeling and deep thought, made possible by deep study of the means to express it; and secondly, that literature, which through the earlier part of last century never received in Ireland the laborious brooding care without which no considerable work of art is possible, now receives increasingly the artist's labour; and consequently that among our later humorists we find a faculty of mirth that lies deeper, reaches farther, judges more subtly, calls into light a wider complex of relations. After all, laughter is the most distinctive faculty of man; and I submit that, so far as literature shows, we Irish can better afford to be judged by our laughter now than a century ago.

1901.

I

THE SHANACHY

HERE is nothing better known about Ireland than this fact : that illiteracy is more frequent among the Irish Catholic peasantry than in any other class of the British population; and that especially upon the Irish-speaking peasant does the stigma lie. Yet it is, perhaps, as well to inquire a little more precisely what is meant by an illiterate. If to be literate is to possess a knowledge of the language, literature, and historical traditions of a man's own country—and this is no very unreasonable application of the word— then this Irish-speaking peasantry has a better claim to the title than can be shown by most bodies of men. I have heard the existence of an Irish literature denied by a roomful of prosperous educated gentlemen; and, within a week, I have heard, in the same county, the classics of that literature recited by an Irish peasant who could neither write nor read. On which part should the stigma of illiteracy set the uglier brand?

The Gaelic revival sends many of us to school in Irish-speaking districts, and, if it did nothing else, at least it would have sent us to school in pleasant places among the most lovable preceptors. It was a blessed change from London to a valley among hills that look

over the Atlantic, with its brown stream tearing down
among boulders, and its heathy banks, where the keen
fragrance of bog-myrtle rose as you brushed through
in the morning on your way to the head of a pool.
Here was indeed a desirable academy, and my preceptor matched it.   A big, loose-jointed old man,
rough, brownish-gray all over, clothes, hair, and face;
his cheeks were half-hidden by the traditional close-
cropped whisker, and the rest was an ill-shorn stubble.
Traditional, too, was the small, deep-set, blue eye, the
large, kindly mouth, uttering English with a soft
brogue, which, as is always the case among those
whose real tongue is Irish, had no trace of vulgarity.
Indeed, it would have been strange that vulgarity of
any sort should show in one who had perfect manners, and the instinct of a scholar, for this preceptor
was not even technically illiterate.   He could read
and write English, and Irish, too, which is by no
means so common; and I have not often seen a man
happier than he was over Douglas Hyde's collection
of Connacht love-songs, which I had fortunately
brought with me.   But his main interest was in history—that history which had been rigorously excluded
from his school training, the history of Ireland.   I
would go on ahead to fish a pool, and leave him poring
over Hyde's book; but when he picked me up,
conversation went on where it broke off—somewhere
among the fortunes of Desmonds and Burkes, O'Neills
and O'Donnells.   And when one had hooked a large
sea-trout, on a singularly bad day, in a place where no
sea-trout was expected, it was a little disappointing
to find that Charlie's only remark, as he swept the net
under my capture, was: " The Clancartys was great

men too. Is there any of them living?" The scholar
in him had completely got the better of the sportsman.

Beyond his historic lore (which was really considerable, and by no means inaccurate) he had many songs
by heart, some of them made by Carolan, some by
nameless poets, written in the Irish which is spoken
to-day.   I wrote down a couple of Charlie's lyrics
which had evidently a local origin; but what I sought
was one of the Shanachies who carried in his memory
the classic literature of Ireland, the epics or ballads of
an older day. Charlie was familiar, of course, with
the matter of this " Ossianic " literature, as we all
are, for example, with the story of Ulysses. He knew
how Oisin dared to go with a fairy woman to her own
land; how he returned in defiance of her warning;
how he found himself lonely and broken in a changed
land; and how, in the end, he gave in to the teaching
of St. Patrick (" Sure how would he stand up against
it?" said Charlie), and was converted to Christ.   But
all the mass of rhymed verse which relates the dia-
logues between Oisin and Patrick, the tales of Finn
and his heroes which Oisin told to the Saint, the fierce
answers with which the old warrior met the Gospel
arguments—all this was only vaguely familiar to him.
I was looking for a man who had it by heart.

The search for the repositories of this knowledge
leads sometimes into strange contrasts. One friend
of mine lay stretched for long hours on top of a roof
of sticks and peat-scraws which was propped against
the wall of a ruined cabin, while within the evicted
tenant, still clinging to his home as life clings to the
shattered body, lay bedridden on a lair of rushes, and
chanted the deeds of heroes; his voice issuing through

the vent in the roof, at once window and chimney, from the kennel in which was neither room nor light for a man to sit and record the verses. My own chance was luckier and happier. It came on a day when a party of us had set out in quest of a remote mountain lough. Our way led along the river, and as we drove up to where the valley contracted, and the tillage land decreased in extent and fertility, the type of the people changed. They were Celts and Catholics, evident to the least practised eye. A little further still from civilisation we reached the fringe that was Gaelic not merely in blood; the kindly woman whose cottage warmed and sheltered us when we returned half-foundered from plunging through bogs was an Irish speaker. She had no songs herself, but if I wanted them her neighbour, James Kelly, was the best of company, and would keep me listening the length of a night.

I pushed my bicycle through a drizzle of misty rain up the road over mountainous moor, before I saw his cottage standing trim and white under its thatch in a screen of trees, and as I was nearing it, the boy with me showed me James down in a hollow, filling a barrow with turf. He stopped work as I came down, and called off his dog, looking at me curiously enough, for, indeed, strangers were a rarity in that spot, clean off the tourist track, and away from any thoroughfare. One's presence had to be explained out of hand, and I told him exactly why I had come. He looked surprised and perhaps a little pleased, that his learning should draw students. But he made no pretence of ignorance; the only question was, how he could help me. Did I want songs of the modern kind, or the older songs of Finn Mac-Cool? If it was the latter, it seemed I was not well able to manage the common talk, and these songs were written in " very hard Irish, full of ould strong words."

I should like to send the literary Irishmen of my acquaintance one by one to converse with James Kelly as a salutary discipline. He was perfectly courteous, but through his courtesy there pierced a kind of toleration that carried home to one's mind a profound conviction of ignorance. People talk about the servility of the Irish peasant. Here was a man who professed his inability to read or write, but stood perfectly secure in his sense of superior education. His respect for me grew evidently when he found me familiar with the details of more stories than he expected. I was raised to the level of a hopeful pupil. They had been put into English, I told him. "Oh, ay, they would be, in a sort of a way," said James, with a fine scorn. Soon we broke new ground, for James had by heart not only the Fenian or Ossianic cycle, but also the older Sagas of Cuchulain. He confused the cycles, it is true, taking the Red Branch heroes for contemporaries of the Fianna, which is much as if one should make Heracles meet Odysseus or Achilles in battle; but he had these earlier legends by heart, a rare acquirement among the Shanachies of to-day.

Here then was a type of the Irish illiterate. A man somewhere between fifty and sixty, at a guess; of middle height, spare and well-knit, high-nosed, fine-featured, keen-eyed; standing there on his own ground, courteous and even respectful, yet consciously a scholar; one who had travelled too—had worked in England and Scotland, and could tell me that the High-

land Gaelic was far nearer to the language of the old
days than the Irish of to-day; finally, one who could
recite without apparent effort long narrative poems in
a dead literary dialect.   When I find an English work-
man who can stand up and repeat the works of
Chaucer by heart, then and not till then I shall see an
equivalent for James Kelly.

And yet it would be a different thing entirely.
Chaucer has never survived in oral tradition.   But
in the West of Donegal, whence James Kelly's father
emigrated to where I found his son, every old person
had this literature in mind, and my friend was no
exception.   It is among the younger generation, who
have been taught in the National Schools (surely the
most ironic of all titles), that the language and the history of the nation are dying out.   Yet that is changing.
For instance, James Kelly's son reads and writes
Irish, and on another day helped me to note down
some of his father's lore.

For it was late when I came first to the house, and
though the Shanachie pressed me (not knowing even
my name) to stay the night, I had to depart for that
day, after I had heard him recite in the traditional
chant some staves of an Ossianic lay, and sing to the
traditional air Carolan's famous lyric, " The Lord of
Mayo."   We drank a glass of whisky from my flask,
a cup of tea that his wife made; and as we went into
the house he asked a favour in a whisper.   It was
that I should eat plenty of his good woman's butter.
He escorted me a good way over the hill, for, said
he, when I had come that far to see him, it was the
least that he should put me a piece on my road, and
he exhorted me to come again for " a good crack

together." And if I deferred visiting him for another
year that was largely because I did not like to face
again this illiterate without acquiring a little more
knowledge.

What came of my second visit must be written in
another paper. But here, let it be understood this is
no exceptional case. In every three or four parishes
along the Western seaboard and for twenty miles
inland, from Donegal to Kerry, there is the like of
James Kelly to be found. It may be that in another
fifty years not one of these Shanachies will linger;
education will have made a clean sweep of illiteracy.
And yet again, it may be that by that time, not only
in the Western baronies but through the length and
breadth of Ireland, both song and story and legend
will be living again on the lips and in the hearts of
the people. *Go leigidh Dia sin.*

II

THE LIFE OF A SONG

THERE was a great contention some years ago fought out in a law court between the British Museum and the Royal Irish Academy, for the custody of certain treasure trove, gold vessels and ornaments disinterred on an Irish beach. The treasures went back, as was only right, to Ireland, where is a rich storehouse of such things, for the soil has been dug over in search for the material relics of ancient art. Yet little heed has been paid to treasures of far greater worth and interest, harder to sell, it is true, but easier to come by—the old songs and stories which linger in oral tradition or in old manuscripts handed down from peasant to peasant. Only within the last few years did the Irish suddenly awake to a consciousness that the authentic symbols, or, rather, the indisputable proofs of the national existence so dear to them, were slipping out of their hands. So far had the heritage perished, so ill had the tradition been maintained, that when they turned to revive their expiring language and literature, the first question asked was, " What is it you would revive? Was there ever a literature in Irish or merely a collection of ridiculous rhodomontade? Is there a language, or

does there survive merely a debased jargon, employed
by ignorant peasants among themselves, and chiefly
useful, like a thieves' lingo, to baffle the police?"

These were the questions put, and not one in a thousand of Irish Nationalists could give an answer according to knowledge.

Now, matters are changed.   The books that were
available in print have been read; the work of poets
extant only in manuscript has been printed and widely
circulated; the language is studied with zeal, and not
in Ireland only, but wherever Irishmen are gathered.
Yet nothing has so strongly moved me to believe that
we cherish the living rather than pay funeral honours
to the dead, as certain hours spent with a peasant who
could neither write nor read.

The life of a song—poets have said it again and
again in immortal verse—is of all lives the most endur-
ing.   Kingdoms pass, buildings crumble, but the work
which a man has fashioned " out of a mouthful of
air " defies the centuries; it keeps its shape and its
quivering substance.   Strongest of all such lives are
perhaps those where " the mouthful of air " is left by
the singer mere air, and no more, unfixed on paper or
parchment; when the song goes from mouth to mouth,
altering its contours it may be, but unchanged in
essence, though coloured by its immediate surroundings as a flower fits itself to each soil.   Such was the
song that I had the chance to write down, from lips to
which it came through who knows how many generations.

The story which it tells is among the finest in that
great repertory of legend which, since Ireland began to
take count of her own possessions, has become fami-

liar to the world. It is the theme of a play in the last
book published by the chief of modern Irish poets,
Mr. W. B. Yeats. But since he tells the story in a way
of his own, and since it is none too well known even
in those parts of Ireland where its hero's name is
a proverb (*Comh làidir le Cuchulain*, Strong as Cuchulain), it may be well to set out the legend here.

Cuchulain, the Achilles of Irish epic, was famous
from the day in boyhood when he got his name by
killing, bare-handed, the smith's fierce watchdog that
would have torn him. The ransom for the killing was
laid on by the boy himself, and it was that he should
watch Culann's house for a year and a day till a pup
should be grown to take the place of the slain dog.
So he came to be called Cú Chulain, Culann's Hound,
and by that name he was known when, as a young
champion, he set out for the Isle of Skye, where the
warrior-witch Sgathach (from whom the island is
called) taught the crowning feats of arms to all young
heroes who could pass through the ordeals she laid
upon them.

There was no trial that Cuchulain could not support,
and the fame of him drew on a combat with another
Amazonian warrior, Aoifé, who, in the story that I
heard, was Sgathach's daughter, though Lady Gregory in her fine book *Cuchulain of Muirthemne* gives
another version. But, at any rate, Cuchulain defeated
Aoifé, and she gave love to her conqueror—whose
passion for the fierce queen was not strong enough to
keep him from Ireland. When he made ready to go,
the woman warrior told him that a child was to be
born of their embraces, and she asked what should be
done with it. "If it be a girl, keep it," said Cuchu-

lain, " but if a boy, wait till his thumb can fill this
ring "—and he gave her the circlet—" then send him
to me." So he departed, leaving wrath behind him.

The child born was a son, and Aoifé reared him and
taught him all feats of arms that could be taught to a
mortal, except one only, and of that feat only Cuchulain was master : " the way," said James Kelly, pre-
facing his ballad with such an explanation as I am
now giving, " there would be none could kill him but
his own father." And when the boy had learnt all
and was the perfect warrior, Aoifé sent him out to
Ireland under a pledge to refuse his name to any that
should ask it, well knowing how the wardens of the
coast would stop him on the shore. It fell out as she
purposed. The young Connlaoch defeated champion
after champion till Cuchulain himself went down, and
was recognised by his son. But the pledge tied Connlaoch's tongue, and only when he lay dying, slain by
the magic throw which Aoifé had withheld from his
knowledge, could he reveal himself to his father, the
great and childless hero, whose lament for his lost
son is written in the song that I set out to secure, on a
day of sun and rain, last summer, when great soft
clouds drove full sail through the moist atmosphere,
their shadows sweeping over brown moor and green
valley, while far away towards the sea, mountain
peaks rose purple and amethystine in the distance.

Twice before this I had been in the little cottage on
Cark Mountain; first, when the chance rumour heard
in a neighbouring cabin of a man with countless songs
and stories sent me off to investigate; and for a second
time, when I had come back with a slightly better
knowledge of Gaelic and had taken down a few verses

of the poem. These, sent to an Irish scholar, had sufficed to identify the ballad with one printed in Miss Brooke's *Reliques of Irish Poetry,* a characteristic production of the latter days of the eighteenth century, when Macpherson, with his adaptation of the Ossianic poems, and Bishop Percy, with his gathering of old English ballads, had set a fashion soon to culminate in Scott's great achievement.

They proved, however, not identity only but difference; and the ballad as I have it in full with its nineteen quatrains, is even less like the longer version given by O'Halloran to Miss Brooke, than the opening stanzas suggested. In them the variations were mainly textual, and when I read out O'Halloran's version to James Kelly, his son, a keen listener, declared a preference for the printed text. But the old man was of another mind. " It's the same song," he said, " sure enough, but there's things changed in it, and I know rightly about them. Some one was giving it the way it would be easier to understand, leaving out the old hard words. And I did that myself once or twice the last day you were here, and I was vexed after, when I would be thinking about it. And this day you will be to take down what I say, let you understand it or not; just word for word, the right way it should be spoken."

There you have in a glimpse the custodian of legend. The man was illiterate, technically, but he knew by instinct, as his ancestors had known before him, that he was the guardian of the life of a song; he recognised that it was a scripture which he had no right to mutilate or alter. He had to the full that respect for a work of literature which is the best indication of a scholar, and for him at least the line was unbroken from the Ireland of heroes and minstrels to the hour when he chanted over the poem that some bard in the remote ages had fashioned.

Little wonder, too, for his own way of life was close to that of the Middle Ages. Below in the valley, where the Swilly River debouches into its sea lough, was a prosperous little town with banks and railway; but to reach the bleak brown moor where James Kelly's house stood, you must climb by one of two roads, each so rough and steep that a bicycle cannot be ridden down them. Here, in a little screen of scrub alders, stands the cottage, where three generations of the family live together. His own home consisted simply of two rooms with no upper story, but it was trim and comfortable, the dresser well filled, and the big pot over the turf fire gave out a prosperous steam. The son, a grown man, waited from his turf-cutting to help in our discussion; the wife was abroad that day, and one daughter was just starting for market with a web of homespun cloth which they had dressed in the household. The spinning wheel stood in the corner; but another girl was busy near the fire with more modern work, hemming shirts with a machine for a Derry factory, and the bleached linen was the only thing in the house which had not taken on the brown tints of peat smoke.

James Kelly himself, as he sat by the fire declaiming at me, was all browns and greys, like the country outside his door; and his eyes were like brown streams running through that peaty mountain, with their movement and sparkle, and their dark depths. At other times easy, like that of all Irish peasants, his manner

changed and grew rough and imperious when the
business began. I must not interrupt with questions.
I must write down, syllable for syllable, that the song
might be got " the right way." It was by no means
easy to carry out these directions, for the poem was
written in an Irish not spoken to-day, as unlike as the
Chaucerian English is to our common speech; and
even to write down modern Irish by ear I was poorly
qualified. Things were made harder, too, by the
manner of recitation, as traditional as the words. He
chanted, with a continuous vocalisation, and while he
chanted, elbow and knee worked like a fiddler's or
piper's marking the time. However, with persistence,
I got the thing down, letting him first say a verse fully
through, then writing line by line or as near as I
could; then going back and asking questions in detail:
the son coming to my rescue, when the old man lost
patience (as he did once in every ten minutes) and
interposing usefully in our discussions.

For there were endless discussions as to the meaning of words, and nothing could be more curious than
to see the old man's endeavour to give in English not
merely a bare rendering, but the colour of every
phrase. It made me realise as nothing else could
have done, how fine was his feeling for the shade of
a word, and I cannot describe his dissatisfaction with
the poor equivalents he could find. He was happy
enough when the debate drifted into an exposition—
always addressed to his son—of the uses of some rare
word in the Irish, the manner of exposition being by
citation of passages from other songs, or phrases that
might occur in talk. I have listened to many a professor doing the same thing in Greek and Latin, but

E

to none who had a finer instinct for the business.
Kelly's vexation came when he had to "put English
on" a word for me, and the obvious equivalent was
not the right one.   Sometimes I could help; sometimes
he arrived by himself at what satisfied him, though
once at least it was droll enough.   We were at the
lines where Connlaoch, dying, says to his father: "If
I could give my secret to any under the sun, it is to
your bright body I would tell it."   The trouble was
about the phrase "bright body," for the word "cneas"
means literally "skin," but is used (just like $\chi\rho\acute{\omega}s$
in Homer) to signify "person."   What James wanted
to convey to me was that the word was not the common one for "body," and at last he smote his thigh.
"Carkidge," he cried, "it's carkidge (carcase), 'It is
to your clear carkidge I would tell it.'"   A man with
less instinct for literature would have said "body"
at once, and never trouble more; but James knew at
once too much and too little, and I give the instance
to show how an Irishman unlettered in English may
be deeply imbued with the true spirit of letters through
a literature of his own.

There were, however, several passages where I
could get no clear account of the meaning, and in
some I have since found by comparison with the text
which O'Halloran provided for Miss Brooke that Kelly
had got the words twisted.   For instance, the first
stanza opens simply :—

> " There came to us a stout champion,
> The hearty champion Connlaoch."

But of the next two lines I could get no clearer rendering than that "he just came in full through these

people for diversion and for fun to himself." Then
the ballad continues at once—for its method is terse
and its transitions abrupt throughout—to give us the
words of the men who meet Connlaoch on his land-
ing :—

> " Where have you been, O tender gallant,
> Riding like a noble's son?
> Methinks by the way of your coming,
> You are wandering or astray."

And Connlaoch answers the taunt and the challenge
implied :—

> " My coming is over seas from the land
> Of the High King of the World,
> To prove my merry prowess
> Athwart the high chiefs of Erin."

(It seemed to me characteristic that the stock epithet
of valour should be " merry " or " laughing.") The
ballad added no reply (though in Miss Brooke's version at this point there is a dialogue of warnings), but
went on to tell in the shortest possible words how
Conall Cearnach (" the Victorious ") rode out from
Emain Macha and met the challenger :—

> " Out started Conall, not weak of hand,
> To get news of the noble's son.
> Bitter and hard was the way of it;
> Conall was tied by Connlaoch."

> " ' Bring word from us to Hound's head,'
> Said the King in fierce sullen tones,
> To Dundalk sunny and bright,
> To the Hound, Dog's jaw."

Then Cuchulain (thus described by versions of the
nickname won when he broke the jaws of Culann's
hound) made answer :—

" Hard for us is hearing of the captivity
Of the man whose plight is told ;
And hard it is to try the venom of blades
With the warrior that bound Conall.''

But the messenger pleads :—

" Do not think but to go to the rescue
Of the destroying keen dangerous warrior,
Of the hand that had no fear for any,
To loose him, and he fettered.''

Then (as Miss Brooke in the majestic manner of the eighteenth century puts it) :—

" Then with firm step and dauntless air,
Cucullin went and thus the foe addrest,
Let me, O valiant knight (he cried),
        Thy courtesy request,
To me thy purpose and thy name confide.''

And so on through a sonorous description of dialogue and fight till :—

" At length Cucullin's kindling soul arose,
Indignant shame recruited fury lends ;
With fatal aim his glittering lance he throws,
And low on earth the dying youth extends.''

Or, as I translate almost literally from James Kelly's version, which is considerably briefer than the text which Miss Brooke has so volubly expanded :—

" Out set the Hound of the keen, smooth blade
To see the work that Conall made,
Till he pierced with a bitter blow,
That hero youth his hardy foe.''

That is all we are told of the fighting ; the ballad passes straight to a terse dramatic dialogue, which Cuchulain opens :—

> " Champion, tell your story,
> For I see your wounds are heavy:
> 'Twill be short ere they raise your cairn,
> So hide your testament no longer."

" That's what he said to the son," said James Kelly, finishing the verse, and beginning afresh,

> " Let me fall on my face,
> For methinks 'tis you are my father,
> And for fear lest men of Eiré should see
> Me retreating from your fierce grapple."

" Then," said James, " the son spoke for to tell him the reason he couldn't spake at the first " :—

> " I took pledges to my mother
> Not to give my story to any single man,
> If I would give it to any under the sun,
> It is to your bright body I would tell it."

(" Complimenting him, like," said James.) Then he recited the stanza which tells by implication how in the long duel Cuchulain was at last driven to use the irresistible stroke of Sgathach's teaching :—

> " I lay my curse on my mother,
> That she put me under pledge;
> But if it were not for the feat of magic
> I had not been got for nothing."

(It is a fine phrase surely, " You had paid dear in blood before you mastered me.")

Cuchulain answers groaning, with a wail for the lineage that is cut off :

> " I lay my curse on your mother,
> For she destroyed a multitude of young ones;
> And because the treachery that was in her
> Left your smooth flesh reddened."

Then comes, with the boy's dying word, the revelation of the most tragic moment in the fight.

> " Cuchulain, beloved father,
>   Is it not a wonder you did not know me
>   When I cast my spear crooked and feebly
>   Against your bush of blades.''

Where will you find a finer stroke of invention?
The boy, tongue-tied by his pledge, knows his father
and feels his defence failing against the terrible onset;
he would not, if he could, be the victor, but he thinks
of a way within the honour of his bond which may
awaken knowledge of him; and he casts his javelin
with a clumsiness not to be looked for in the champion
" that tied Conall." It is useless, the battle madness
is in Cuchulain, he thinks only of conquest, an end to
the supple, quick parrying, and he throws the gaebulg,
a spear of dragon's bones bristling with points (his
" bush of blades "), with the magic cast that there is
no meeting. And now there is nothing left to him but
the lamentation,

> " Och, och ! Great is my madness !
>   I lifting here my young lad !
>   My son's head in my one hand,
>   His arms and his raiment on the other.

> I, the father that slew his son,
>   May I never throw spear nor noble javelin;
>   The hand that slew its son,
>   May it win torture and sharp wounding.

> " The grief for my son I put from me never,
>   Till the flagstones of my side crumble,
>   It is in me, and through my heart,
>   Like a sharp blaze in the hoar hill grasses.

" If I and my heart's Connlaoch
Were playing our kingly feats together,
We could range from wave to shore
Over the five provinces of Erin."

The penultimate stanza, with its magnificent closing
image and its truly Æschylean hyperbole, is not even
suggested in Miss Brooke's version.   It is, perhaps,
the finest thing in the poem; but I hardly know any
ballad finer as a piece of dramatic narrative; and the
resonant verse, strongly rhymed (in the Gaelic asso-
nances), and copiously stressed with alliteration, bears
out the theme.

These, I trust, are critical opinions.   But if the col-
lector would have a special weakness for a vase which
his own spade had unearthed, I may be prejudiced in
favour of the poem, which I got in the sweat of my
brow from very probably the one man living who
knew it in that form.

Tellers of old Irish fairy tales about enchanted
princes, magic cocks and hens, and the like, are still
numerous; but it is very rare to find a man who keeps
living the old poetry which was made, perhaps, in the
twelfth century.   Yet while any survive the tradition
is still there; the song still lives, for I did not spend
my hours without feeling that this old man could
respond to any emotion that the song-maker put into
the sound and the meaning and the associations of his
words.   There are still those to whom the Irish even
of the twelfth century is no dead language.   Even if it
were, no doubt the songs made in it might still be
strong in life, as are to-day those of Homer and a
hundred others.   But in the case of these smaller
literatures, once the tongue itself has ceased to be

heard, dumbness and paralysis fall upon what might else be so full of vitality. And a song has more than its own life, it has power to quicken, to breed. If any one considers that legend of the son and father (found in many languages, yet in none, I think, more finely shaped), it is easy to see how from age to age it may revive itself in new forms, entering into other shapes, as Helen's figure adorns not her own story only, but the praise of a thousand women. Let it be understood that this legend is only one of a cycle, and that the song which I wrote down was only the barest fraction of James Kelly's repertory. Indeed, he was vexed that I should take it as a specimen, for he himself " had more conceit in " the lays that tell of Finn and his companions, and I could have filled a volume, and maybe several volumes, from his recitations.

These songs may die, the language may die, the Irish race may be swallowed up in England and America. But it is my belief that the strong intellectual life which made of Ireland a home of the arts before the Normans came across channel may, like many another life in nature, spring after centuries of torpor into vigour and fertility again. That is the belief and hope of many of us; but nothing has rendered me so confident in it as to find this work of a strong and fine art not laid aside and neglected, but honoured and current to-day, and, though in a poor man's cottage, living with as full a life as when it was chanted at the feasts of princes.

IRISH EDUCATION AND IRISH CHARACTER.

EDUCATION in Ireland has been organised by the State in accordance with English ideas. Had English influence been able to bring about any large measure of conformity between the two countries, there would have been little or no need for a separate paper on moral training in Irish schools. But what conformity there is, is purely superficial; and although free development has been hindered, and Irish institutions for teaching are less characteristic than they would have been if entirely left to themselves, still the moral influences which emerge wherever pupils and teachers are brought together reveal themselves in Ireland, and reveal themselves as Irish. The object of this paper, then, is to illustrate, so far as possible, the nature and the symptoms of these distinctive influences.

First of all, it may be said broadly that no ordinary person in Ireland contemplates the possibility of teaching morality apart from religion; and by religion is meant emphatically this or that particular creed. Almost every school maintained by the State is managed locally by a clergyman, who appoints the teacher, and public feeling is so strong on the matter that in any neighbourhood even a small group of families of any particular denomination is always provided with a separate school of its own. Of late, indeed, opinion has begun to agitate for associating the laity with the clergy in the management of schools;

but this does not indicate any desire to lessen the importance given to the part played by religion in education.

Further, so far as Catholic Ireland is concerned, an immense proportion of the teaching both in primary and secondary schools is done by members of religious orders, and in these, of course, there is no conception of separating moral influences from religious. There is, however, no evidence known to me that even in the few Protestant schools which are partly or wholly under lay control any duties, other than those of ordinary school work, are inculcated except as part of a Christian's religious obligations. This entire state of things is due to the fact that positive Christian belief, and the practice of religious observances, are everywhere in Ireland very general, and among the Catholic population almost universal. It is also hardly necessary to point out that in many respects the standard of Irish morality is so high that the example of Ireland may be quoted with confidence in support of the view which makes moral teaching necessarily a part of religion.

But from such broad generalities there is not much to be gathered, and I proceed to examine in some detail the existing institutions—beginning at the top with higher education.

It follows from what has been said that, in the general opinion of Irishmen, there can be no positive moral influence where there is no religious teaching; and for that reason a university without a school of theology or arrangements for corporate worship is, to Irishmen, a university deficient in moral safeguards. This accounts for the fact that Catholic opinion was much less opposed to the Protestant University of Dublin than to the more modern Queen's Colleges, which, designed by England to provide for her wants of Ireland, excluded religion entirely from their purview. This provision satisfied no one, except to some extent the Presbyterians, who accepted Queen's College, Belfast, with some alacrity, though in practice demanding that its head should always be a staunch professor of their own persuasion. But Catholics as a body refused to accept either the University of Dublin with its Protestant atmosphere or the " godless " Queen's Colleges; and since Ireland is mainly a Catholic country, and the National University has not yet created a tradition, it is clear that not much can be gleaned on the subject of Irish ideas of moral training from Irish universities.

Yet Trinity College is well worth study, for in it we have a free growth, typifying both in its virtues and in its defects the ruling Protestant class, landed and professional. Here, unquestionably, the chief moral influence is that of the Church, felt, as at Oxford, directly through the chapel services and sermons, and indirectly through the presence of a large body of theological students. The second of these influences is specially strong in Dublin, because these students have an organisation of their own in the University Theological Society, and also because the work of the Divinity School at Dublin comprises much that is done in England by the training colleges. I should therefore be inclined to put the positive influence of dogmatic religion higher at Dublin than at Oxford.

On the other hand, the vaguer humanitarian enthusiasms which are more or less allied to Socialism, and with which the High Church party willingly allies itself, have, I think, much less hold in Trinity than at the English universities; though the movement which sends so many brilliant young Englishmen into work (temporary or permanent) in the East End of London has its parallel in the recently organised Social Service Society, which attempts something for the reclamation of Dublin slums.   Again, in regard to more definitely political aspirations, Irish Protestants are somewhat unfortunately situated.   Trinity as a whole has no sympathy with the ideals that appeal to Ireland as a nation, and it always seems to lack first-hand touch with the best English thought, whether Liberal or Tory.   This isolation from the main movement of Irish thought and feeling on the one hand, and on the other, this enforced separation from the current of English life, keep the place a little old-fashioned; and to generate enthusiasm, ideals and feelings need a certain freshness.   If it be held (as I should hold) that a university's main moral function is to produce enthusiasts rather than merely decent citizens, in this respect, I think, Trinity fails.

In regard to the less direct influences, a good deal may be noted.   The general trend of life in Trinity is towards frugality, just as at Oxford it is towards extravagance.   Consequently, money is less of an advantage, poverty less of a drawback than at the English universities; the standard of living is more uniform; and in the society of which the university is typical, and which it influences, respect for wealth as wealth is noticeably rare.   Again, the idea of education is more disciplinary than in England.   Irishmen go to college, not to acquire culture by contact, but to learn certain definite things; and the university, in its anxiety to find out if the task is being learnt, multiplies examinations. The same idea pervades all Irish education—the old-fashioned demand for a positive result in knowledge; and if it leads to an excessive value set upon these tests, it also goes far to discourage idleness.

In another matter Trinity College is typical of Irish ideas generally. Games are simply taken as games, not as a main business of life in which success may even have a marketable value. Everybody recognizes their physical use, and more than that, their use as a means of bringing men together. But nobody in Ireland, save here and there a stray apostle of English notions, talks of the moral lessons to be acquired by fielding out or by patient batting. Compulsory games at school are practically unknown; nobody plays unless he wants to; so that the duffer does not experience the questionable moral advantage of physical discomfort and frequent humiliation, and the naturally painstaking or excellent athlete gets no more than his fair chance of exercising his gifts. And these are less likely to have an undue importance in their possessor's eyes, because they will not of themselves lead him to a position of great distinction in an Irish university.

Unfortunately, Trinity College is the only place in Ireland—unless perhaps a saving clause should be made for Queen's College, Belfast—which offers what is meant by a university life. The National University, whether in Dublin, Cork or Galway, brings young men together only in classes and in one or two debating societies. Yet even so, I question whether, in some ways, life does not beat stronger in it than in

Trinity; whether the moral influences proper to a university, the enthusiasm, the contagion of generous ideas, are not here more strongly felt.   The reason for this view must be given.

Trinity has never been the University of Ireland. It is ceasing to be the University of Protestant Ireland, for Protestants, who can afford to do so, send their sons increasingly to Oxford or Cambridge, and Trinity, which has not known how to create a true and special function for itself, is becoming merely a cheap substitute for these English institutions.   And the reason for this is a moral reason which goes to the root of many questions connected with Irish education. Should Irish schools and colleges seek to educate citizens for the Empire, or citizens for Ireland? During the last half century, while the Imperialist idea has been developing in England, Trinity has thrown all its moral weight into support of that idea.   But the Imperialist idea in England is very different from the same idea as viewed in Canada or New Zealand or Australia; and universities in these countries address themselves particularly to local needs.   In the section of Ireland which Trinity represents, local patriotism is held to conflict with Imperial patriotism, and one has to observe that Trinity's Imperialism is forwarding tendencies which are leaving her drained.   Nationalists may respect the sincerity of convictions so pressed in defiance of a local interest; but a university, whose main emotional appeal is directed towards evoking primarily an enthusiasm for England, cannot be of much use to Nationalist Ireland.   Catholics may (and do) respect the thoroughness of the religious teaching, and the strong grip which Protestantism keeps on the university; but a university which inculcates morals through a Protestant religion is not precisely suitable to Catholics.   Yet Catholics and Nationalists alike infinitely prefer a university or a college or a school with strong Protestant beliefs, or strong Imperialist patriotism, to an institution with neither beliefs nor patriotism at all.   The colourless and merely scholastic ideals of the Queen's Colleges, and the huge examining machinery known as the Royal University, typified in their total lack of moral influences all that was worst in the educational system under which Ireland labours.

I pass to a brief examination of the boarding schools, institutions which have never flourished in Ireland. Nearly all Protestants and many Catholics, if they can afford it, send their sons to England to be taught. The ideals of the English Public School have reacted so strongly upon Irish Protestant schools that nothing need be said of these—not one of which has ever, within living memory, had a continuous prosperity. The important Catholic schools are managed by the great teaching orders, especially by the Jesuits, and managed at astonishingly low cost.   They give everywhere more than value for the fees which they receive. No unendowed institution could compete with them; and it practically comes to this, that the regular clergy subsidise education with their own unpaid labour and even with their own funds, in order to maintain their influence over the faith and morals of their country.   Whether it might be more to the advantage of Irish parents to pay more and get something different, is another question; but those of us who least like the exclusive delegation of these important functions to the priesthood, cannot but admire the thoroughness and consistency with which the Catholic priesthood's idea is carried out. It would be hard to overstate the moral effect of that vast organised system of self-sacrifice and self-suppression.

Three or four points may be noted in relation to these schools. One is, that in all classrooms and playgrounds, a master is always present. Comparing this with the system in vogue at many English schools, under which a boy out of school hours is always forced to live in public by rules which compel him either to be playing some game or looking on while others play, I prefer the system of frank supervision, as leaving more individual freedom and choice of pursuits, and as making serious bullying impossible. Generally, the idea that it is good for a boy to be knocked about without stint is foreign to Irish ideas. A pleasant and characteristic feature of Jesuit schools is the habit of telling off some boy to act as companion and cicerone to a newcomer for his first week or fortnight; and the ridiculous English fashion which prescribes that the smallest fag should be described as a " man " is unknown. Christian names, not surnames, are used generally. The unpopularity of boarding schools in Ireland is due to the great value set upon home life; and an Irish boarding school is far less distinct from home life than an English one.

English eyes would be surprised and a good deal shocked by the presence of a billiard table in every playroom; yet it may fairly be argued that it is wise to limit the number of things that have the fascination of the forbidden. A more serious criticism would address itself to the permitted slovenliness. Untidiness amounts to a national vice in Ireland, and, though one may overstate its gravity, the secondary schools could and should do much more to remedy this national defect than they are at present doing. At one first-class Irish establishment—admirably equipped with buildings, playground, and all other appliances—boots used to go unblacked from one end of the month to the other. The boys who come here come largely from the well-to-do farming class, in whose homes, in many ways so pleasant and worthy of respect, there is often a lamentable lack of that charm which comes of notable housewifery. The young men who return from this school will be less apt than they should be to value good housewifery in their wives and mothers.

But of all sinners in this regard the State is the chief offender. Under the Code of the National Board of Education a national schoolmaster or mistress is bound to teach cleanliness and decency by precept and example. He or she is paid an average wage (without allowances) of thirty shillings or one pound a week according to sex; and out of that an appearance befitting superior station has to be maintained—for in Ireland the schoolmaster has always a position of some dignity. For the school the State provides four bare walls, a roof, not always weatherproof, and a few desks. Firing is not provided. Decoration is subject to inspection, and any picture which can be held to have a religious or remotely political bearing is a gross offence against the Code. It follows, in practice, that bare walls are kept bare, though not clean; and let it be remembered that Catholicism, if left to itself, in education always trusts greatly to the appeal to the eye.

F

In every Catholic school uncontrolled by the State the emblems of religion are everywhere present. National schools under State control, even in places where there is not a Protestant child within twenty miles, are rigorously forbidden the use of any such embellishment.   On the other hand, Protestant schools which would gladly, and, as I think, most laudably, furnish themselves with pictures recalling such memories as the shutting of the Derry gates, come under the same tyranny of compromise.   Taste and culture are the expression of an individuality, and individuality is forbidden to Irish teachers in State employ. The State puts a schoolmaster into a schoolhouse, without adequate payment for himself, without adequate provision either for building or the upkeep of building; it bids him to keep it clean, but pays no servant to wash or sweep; and, while enjoining the absence of dirt, it checks and hampers that desire to decorate, which is the positive side of order and taste. The result is, broadly, slatternly schools.

There could hardly be a better moral influence in Ireland than tastefully and brightly decorated schools, cleanly kept. But to secure this the State must provide money, and must give individual freedom. Instead of that, it adapts its institution to the lowest standard of living; and the raggedest child out of the dirtiest cottage will probably be in full keeping with his environment when he takes his place in class.

The same tyranny of compromise sterilises the whole teaching on the moral side. Nothing must be taught nywhere which could offend any susceptibility—except in the hour licensed for the teaching of denominational religion. There must be no appeal to Irish

patriotism, whether it be of Protestant or Catholic.
Irish history may not be taught as a subject, and, until
lately, anything bearing on it, however remotely, was
tabooed.   The poem *Breathes there a man with soul
so dead* was struck out of a lesson book, lest it should
encourage sedition.   To-day certain accepted books
on Irish history may be used as readers; the Irish language may be taught, and is taught; and gradually
with these changes new moral influences are coming
in.   Irish children are being encouraged to remember
their nationality.   Yet, meanwhile, the teacher, who
is to instruct them in the duties of a good citizen, is
debarred from taking any part in local politics, from
serving on any local council.   He is forbidden, in
fact, to be himself a good citizen; forbidden to be anything more than the colourless instrument of a system
of compromise and countercheck.   Nothing is more
certain than this, that to get a good teacher you need
a man's whole personality; you must enlist all his
beliefs and his feelings in the exercise of that moral
function of education which can never be fulfilled by
a mere machine for imparting the rudiments.   Man
everywhere, but especially in Ireland, is, as Aristotle
said, a political animal.   The State in Ireland, when
organising education, tries as far as possible to elimi-
nate the man and produce the pedagogue.

Take, for contrast with all this, the purely native
institution, now unhappily extinct, of the old " classi-
cal academies " kept in the country parts of Munster
by private laymen.   In the eighteenth century, and on
into the nineteenth, these men kept alive the tradition
of Irish popular poetry, sometimes with a real gift.
For good or for bad they were persons of character

and of talent, and the last of them is alive, though he keeps school no longer.   He taught boys who had learnt the rudiments at the ordinary national school, and who wished to carry on their studies with a view either to the priesthood or to medicine.   He was paid only by the fees of his scholars, who were either the sons of farmers about him, or of men living at a distance, who sent their children to be part of the family in some farm where they had kinship or acquaintance. Thus existence for these scholars was divided between the home life of a farm and the hours of school. There was, however, a small element of what in Ireland were called " poor scholars "—boys from the less prosperous North and West, who came (sometimes walking the whole journey) to get learning gratis.   To them teaching was never refused, and their board was provided by the farmers, who " would be snatching them from one and other," since they assisted the other children in preparing tasks.

Now, in the school which my friend has described to me, there was no formal teaching of anything but the prescribed subjects.   But literature would be lying about—Haverty's *History of Ireland*, and the Nationalist papers of the day—and the teacher was there always ready to expound and answer questions.   Himself a fighting politician (a member of the Fenian organisation, whose name is still sacred throughout Ireland), he was careful never to draw in or compromise his pupils; but to teach them the story of their country and discuss it with them was part of his natural occupation.   He taught Irish also, the tongue readiest to him, for he held that Irishmen should know their own language; but the essential business of his school was teaching the simple old-fashioned curriculum, Latin, mathematics, and some Greek. Yet because he was a man who loved and valued knowledge for its own sake, and loved and valued literature, it is probable that he gave a more real training to the mind than is achieved by the most modern system of hand and eye culture and the rest of it. He taught neither religion nor morals, but his teaching assumed throughout, what his example showed, that a man should be true and thorough in what he professed to believe, and should be ready at all times to make sacrifices for principle. Such a school had the only moral influence which in Ireland has ever counted for much—the influence of a strong personality, acting in alliance with the influences of a fully realised religion and of an ordered family life.

I sketch a more concrete picture that always rises in my mind with a ray of hope, when I think of education in Ireland. Out of doors, winter twilight falling on a wild landscape within hearing of the Atlantic surf; the man of the house coming out to talk to me, a handsome Irishman of the old school, frieze-clad, with the traditional side whiskers, the humorous eye and mouth. We talked for a while in the cold, then " Gabh i leith isteach," he said, " for I hear you have the Irish." As I paused in the door to phrase the Gaelic salutation, more devout and courteous than would come to my lips in any other tongue, I was astonished at the company gathered in the long low room. Chairs were set by the wide hearth of course, and from one of them the woman of the house rose to greet me; a settle ran along the side wall, and its length was filled with men and women blotted against the dusk background.   But the centre of the picture was a narrow deal table set in the middle of the room, with candles on it, and benches on each side, and on the benches fully ten children busy with books and copies.   "Are these your burden?" I asked in the quaint Irish phrase.   "A share of them," the man answered; and then I understood that some belonged to other neighbours, and that it was a mutual arrangement for friendliness and help.   None of the children budged; there they were, drilled and disciplined at their work, in the middle of the room, while their elders sat and chatted quietly.   I have never seen elsewhere anything which so filled my conception of what a home should be, as that farmhouse in Corcabascinn—so full of order and good governance, yet so free of constraint, so full of welcome, yet so lacking in expense or display.   For, understand, we who were strangers were brought (much against my will) into the state-room or parlour beyond the party wall, and drink was pressed upon us hospitably.   But the neighbours who had come there (and came daily, I fancy) came neither to eat nor drink (unless maybe tea might be brewing) but simply to sit and smoke and talk, and watch that their children got their lessons properly.   And at the end, perhaps before they parted, perhaps when the family was alone, the rosary would be said by the turf fire, that made, winter or summer, the centre of all that pleasant existence.

It is a pity to think of how poorly the National school, to which those children would go with their tasks in the morning, seconds the help which this home life gives it.   Easily could the school—which takes whatever real light it has from the home, just as it depends for warmth on the few turf which scholars bring daily along with their books—reflect sound and fruitful ideas on to the home through the children.   It could teach the children and the parents, not only the political, but the economic history of their own country; it could teach them what has been done in Ireland, what has succeeded, what has failed, and why; it could teach them, who are already proud of being Irish, to have new reasons for their pride; it could teach them, who are already willing to do their best for Ireland, into what channels the driving force of that willingness may be poured.

Outside of definite religion, the only fruitful source of educational ideas connected with the moral order that I see in Ireland is the Gaelic League.   This organisation, founded to save from extinction, and to revive into new prosperity the national language of Ireland, based itself entirely upon a moral appeal. It appealed to Irishmen as they were proud of their race, to save the most distinctive symbol of their nationality; and the appeal met with an extraordinary promptness of response.   But to stimulate and promote the movement, it was found necessary to widen the propaganda.   Irishmen were urged to learn Irish, and to speak Irish because of pride in their country; the same organisation soon began to teach that an Irishman who set an example of drunkenness, or gave an occasion of it, not only sinned against himself, but against his country.   Vulgar and indecent literature was denounced as un-Irish; Irish dances were advocated, not only for their admirable grace and their historic interest, but also because it was held that dances like the waltz, departed from the austere standard of

Irish morality.   Irish men and women were taught to buy goods of Irish manufacture by the people who taught them to learn the language, on the ground that if the Irish nation continued to ebb away out of Ireland, nationality and language must perish together.

Thus through the medium of a propaganda which at first sight would seem merely literary and archæological, many practical issues of life were related to a purely educational purpose.   There is no doubt that the Gaelic League, now a widespread and solidly established organisation, spending on the whole, perhaps, £30,000 or £40,000 a year on its enterprise, has done as much to promote temperance. and to further Irish industries, as it has accomplished in its peculiar task of reviving the old tongue.   Primarily a teaching institution—for each of the League's eight hundred branches exists to hold classes for Irish study—it has linked with the linguistic teaching a moral idea.   The reaction has been mutual, for there is more intelligent thought on the methods of linguistic teaching in the Gaelic League than one would easily find in all the schools and universities of Ireland.   The appeal to pride of race has quickened intelligence no less than enthusiasm.

It is a very remarkable fact, that the great teaching order of the Christian Brothers has taken up the teaching of Irish and generally the Gaelic League's whole propaganda more thoroughly than any other organisation in Ireland; very remarkable, for their practical success is so conspicuous that Protestant clergymen have repeatedly from the pulpit appealed for extra support to Protestant schools whose pupils, as one preacher said in my hearing, were being ousted in all

competition for employment by the lads from the
Christian Brothers' schools. Whatever the post was,
the preacher said, this body of lay Catholics seemed
always to have a candidate specially prepared for it.
One of the greatest institutions in charge of that order
is the industrial school at Artane, near Dublin, where
eight hundred boys are being prepared for different
trades. Every single one of those boys is now being
taught Irish; that is to say, a linguistic training with a
special appeal to the learner's patriotism has been
superimposed on the ordinary rudiments. It is a
great experiment made by enthusiasts who are also
teachers with an intensely practical bent.

It is too early even to forecast the effect which is
likely to be produced upon Irish education generally
by the new university colleges set up under Mr. Bir-
rell's Act. Yet this may be said. Irish education
needs reform from the top downwards, not from the
bottom upwards. It has lacked idealism, and these
universities in which Ireland, whether of the north
or the south, will be free to express its own character,
can and should set up ideals which will govern every
school in the country. Trinity College has been free
to follow its own bent, and its eyes to-day are, in
scriptural phrase, "on the ends of the earth." Primary education, secondary studies, as governed by
the machinery controlled through the Board of Inter-
mediate Education, and university teaching as directed
and rewarded through the Royal University, have all
in the last resort been inspired by Englishmen who
thought it very desirable that Irish boys and girls
should learn to read and write and cipher, and that
young men and young women should equip them-

selves for clerkships in the civil service, but who never for one instant realised that the end of education is divergence not conformity—to elicit, whether from the race or from the individual, a full and characteristic development.   In twenty years perhaps a paper of interest may be written to show the positive results of education upon Irish character.   At present the most noticeable facts are negative, and may be summed up by affirming a total lack of correspondence between the system employed and the needs and qualities of the Irish people.

1907.

THE IRISH GENTRY.

AT the height on the struggle over the Home Rule Bill, there was published a book interesting as the biography of a remarkable individual, but no less interesting as depicting the crucial moment in the history of an aristocracy. Colonel Moore wisely entitles the life of his father simply *An Irish Gentleman*. Versatile, eloquent, quick-tempered and lovable, excessive in generosity, excessive in courage and self-confidence, with the racecourse for his ruling passion and horsemanship for his supreme achievement, George Henry Moore was the paragon of his class. He displayed in the highest degree those qualities on which the Irish gentry prided themselves and which they most admired : he shared the prestige and power of Irish landlords when prestige and power were at their height; and he confronted the decisive hour when he, and men like him, had to choose between the interest of their country and the interest of their class. There he separated himself from his fellows; he parted from all to whom he was bound by ties of immediate advantage, of pleasure, of association, of affection, and he threw in his lot with Ireland. He saw first the moral bankruptcy of his own class, then their widespread financial ruin; and though he helped to break their political power, and in so doing earned the general love of his countrymen, yet the troubles which beset the landlord class did not spare him, and he died, broken-hearted, forty-three years ago, at the beginning of a struggle which is not ended yet. It is well worth while to consider the circumstances of that stormy career.

First a brilliant schoolboy, then an idle law student, George Henry Moore was driven to travel by the complications of a passionate love affair, and he travelled adventurously, being a pioneer of exploration in the Caucasus and Syria. Sketches reproduced in the book show that he could draw no less well than he wrote. Returning to Ireland at the age of twenty-seven, he devoted himself entirely to hunting and racing, and few men were better known on the turf, nor were there even in the West of Ireland more desperate riders than his brother and himself. George Henry was carried off the field at Cahir in 1843 to all appearance dead; he was alive enough to hear discussion as to his burial. Augustus, less lucky, died of a fall he took riding Mickey Free in the Grand National two years later. The brothers were closely bound to each other in affection, and this was a heavy blow to the survivor; but George Moore continued to race, and in 1846 made the coup of his life, winning £10,000 on "Coranna" for the Chester Cup. He sent £1,000 of it home for distribution among his tenants, and there was soon sore need of the money, for that year saw the second and disastrous failure of the potato crop. The Irish Famine made the turning-point in Moore's history, as in that of his class. The catastrophe which brought him into public life and into the service of his country demonstrated, cruelly enough—though this was the least of its cruelties—the futility of the Irish gentry as a whole.

By the shock of his brother's death in 1845 Moore's mind had been turned to serious thoughts. Matter was not lacking. The report of the Devon Commission upon Irish land, joined to the first failure of the potato crop—with its accompaniment of distress and widespread agrarian crime—gave any Irish landlord food for reflection, and in March, 1846, when a vacancy occurred in the representation of Mayo, Moore came forward as a Whig candidate. The whole landlord interest was at his back, but a Repealer opposed him, and O'Connell's influence carried the day. There were fierce encounters, the landlords marching their tenants to the poll under guards of soldiers, the popular side falling upon these escorts and sometimes carrying off the voters—or enabling them to escape. One of Moore's friends, Mr. Browne, afterwards Lord Oranmore, wrote : " I now see we owe our lives to the priests, as they can excite the whole people against us whenever they like. Whatever may be the cause, Ireland needs reconquering."

That was a typical expression of the gentry's view. Plainly Ireland was in rebellion when landlords could no longer carry their tenants to the poll to vote as the landlord directed. Moore however differed from the generality of Irish landlords in one important respect. He was not divided by religion from the people over whom he ruled, and he can never have had Mr. Browne's feeling of aloofness from Ireland as a country which might need reconquering to re-establish the ascendancy of the " English garrison "; nor was it natural to him to distrust the priests as leaders of a separate and subject race.

In the autumn of 1846, when the threat of famine

had become a certainty, Moore came home to Mayo,
where there was grim business to be done.   His
tenants, on an estate running up into the wild Partry
mountains, numbered five thousand souls.   For their
benefit he utilised far more of his winnings on
" Coranna " than the tithe which he had originally
ear-marked; and not one of all these his dependants
died of want in that outlandish region, though in
places far less remote death was ravenous.   He was
chairman of the Relief Board for the whole county,
and slaved at his task—not harder than other landlords in other parts of Ireland.   But his methods were
more drastic, his view of the situation clearer.   Folk
must have rubbed their eyes and perhaps stopped to
think twice when the owner of " Wolfdog," of
" Anonymous," and a score of other famous horses,
wrote, in answer to a request for his annual subscrip-
tion to the local races, that he thought the county of
Mayo " as little fit to be the scene of such festivities
as he to contribute to their celebration."

But Moore did not content himself with mere admini-
stration of relief.   He saw that the English Government was apathetic and incompetent to face so terrible
an affliction, and he took in hand to create within his
own class an organised force of Irish opinion to bind
together the ruling Irishmen for the good of Ireland.
In company with his friend and kinsman, Lord Sligo,
he " travelled through twenty-seven counties and per-
sonally conferred with most of the leading men in Ireland on the urgent necessity of a united effort to save
the sinking people."   The result was that between
sixty and seventy members of Parliament and some
forty peers pledged themselves to endeavour to secure

united .action upon measures regarding Ireland in the
new session.   On the 14th of January, 1847, the Irish
landlord class held such a muster as had not been
seen since the Union.   " Nearly twenty peers, more
than thirty members of Parliament, and at least six
hundred gentlemen of name and station took part in
it.   The meeting called on Government to prohibit
export of food stuffs and to sacrifice any sum that
might be required to save the lives of the people."
It passed thirty resolutions without dissension; and
then some one asked what was to be done if the
Government refused to adopt any of their suggestions.
Would Irish members then unite to vote against the
Government?   To this, Irish members refused to
pledge themselves, and Moore, as he said afterwards,
" saw at a glance that the confederacy had broken
down."

That was the end of the revolt of the Irish gentry.
It was really the decisive moment of their failure; dis-
organised and futile, they went down by scores in the
ruin of the Encumbered Estates Court, while their
tenants were marking with their bones a road across
the Atlantic.   As for the landlords who were popular
leaders, within a few months after that great assembly,
Daniel O'Connell, who had proposed the first resolu-
tion, died in Rome, heart-broken.   A few months
more and Smith O'Brien, the mover of another reso-
lution, headed a rebellion in sheer despair.

Smith O'Brien had twenty years of parliamentary
life behind him when he was driven to the wild protest
of insurrection.   Twenty years of the same experience
were to bring Moore to a very similar attitude; but in
1847 Moore was hopeful of building up in Parliament

the nucleus of an Independent Irish Party.   When the dissolution came, in 1847, he stood for a second time, but as an Independent, and his work in the famine times carried at least its recognition.   Every single elector who went to the poll gave one of his two votes to the Independent.   He went to Westminster and denounced with equal energy the agrarian murders, which were then rife in Ireland, and those organs of publicity in England which sought to magnify these outrages into an indictment against the Irish nation.   The ferment of indignation against English methods had not yet died out in the hearts of Irish landlords.   Lord Sligo, writing to Moore concerning the controversy which followed, used these words : " I believe that *The Times* did much to cause the feeling which resulted in landlord and parson shooting; it will end by turning us all into Repealers."   If only it had ! But Moore got no help from the landlord class, and the well-to-do Catholic professional men with whom he was principally allied proved themselves unable to resist the temptations of office and of personal interest. In the days of Sadleir and Keogh he fought a desperate fight against Whig place-seekers; his reward was to be finally unseated (in 1857) on an election petition, the charge being that spiritual intimidation had been exercised on his behalf by the priests.   As Colonel Moore observes, if a landlord threatened his tenants with disfavour, which meant eviction, that was " only a legitimate exercise of their rights of property "; but if a priest told his flock that a man would imperil his soul by selling his vote or prostituting it to the use of a despot, the candidate whom that priest supported would lose his seat and be disqualified for re-election.

From this time onward George Henry Moore found himself heading the same way as Smith O'Brien had gone. In 1861 he told the Irish people that if they desired freedom they must take a lesson from Italy; they must " become dangerous "; and he advocated the formation of a new Irish volunteer force to emulate that of 1782. Nothing came of this; but after the American war a new movement grew up, not this time among the landlords or the professional men, nor countenanced by the priests, but nursed in the fierce heart of the people. Ireland had become dangerous. Colonel Moore recognises rightly the difference between the Fenian organisation and the Young Ireland movement which had preceded it. Both were idealistic, but the idealism of 1848 was " the inspiration of a few literary gentlemen, poets, and writers." Smith O'Brien, its titular head, was influenced profoundly by the aristocratic conception of his rightful place as representing the Kings of Thomond. Fenianism was democratic; it was officered largely by men who had themselves fought in the most stubborn of modern wars and who had seen what Irish regiments could do in the citizen levies of Federals and Confederates. It was spontaneous, and it was strong; the measure of its strength is given not by the few flickering outbreaks easily suppressed, but by the terror which it inspired, and by the change which it wrought in the spirit of the people. Moore when he took the step, extraordinary for a man in his position, of enrolling himself in that sworn and secret conspiracy can hardly have failed to foresee the collapse of Fenianism as a fighting force; but he recognised that (in his son's words) " the old complacent toleration of

G

schemers and dishonest politicians had vanished and a sturdy independence had taken its place."

With the advent of that spirit the power of the Irish landlords was doomed. They had made their choice; when they might have made common cause with the whole people of Ireland they had refused to rise beyond their immediate personal advantage and the interests of their class. Moore, who was of themselves, who shared all their pleasures, who loved them, was forced to take a hand in their overthrow. From 1858 onward he had been almost entirely out of politics, living the life of a popular country gentleman, racing and hunting more successfully than ever; his most famous horse, "Croagh Patrick," ran in the 'sixties. But in 1868 he flung all this aside, sold his horses, and undertook to fight the alliance of Whig and Tory which had dominated County Mayo in the landlord interest for ten years.

I shall have the question settled (he said) whether one lord shall drive a hundred human souls to the hustings, another fifty, another a score; whether this or that squire shall call twenty, or ten, or five as good men as himself " his voters " and send them up with his brand on their backs to vote for an omadhaun at his bidding.

He did settle it. Mayo beat the landlords then, and Mayo became the cradle of popular movements ever after. This most typical of Irish land-owning gentlemen had been forced to sever himself from his class and even to injure his class, and it was not by advocacy of self-government that he estranged so close a friend as Lord Sligo. Fintan Lalor's policy, rejected by the Young Irelanders in 1846, was beginning to take hold in 1868; the movement for self-government was becoming linked on to the driving force of land-hunger. In the eyes of Lord Sligo and all his class Tenant Right meant Landlord Wrong, and Moore himself was not exempt from that feeling. He suffered indeed, for rents that he had reduced to a figure fixed by the tenants' own arbitrators were withheld from him. Yet he knew clearly that it was necessary for the country, and not more necessary than just, to secure the tenants in their holdings. No one disputes now that he was right. But the last thing he desired was to abolish the landlords. If they did not like the leadership of the priests " they have," he said, " a remedy left; let them make themselves more popular than the priests. If the landlords will make common cause with the people, the people will make common cause with them." There was never a truer word spoken, but it fell on closed ears.

Moore himself broke the landlords' power at the polls; their infinitely greater power, proceeding from control of the land, was broken by another Mayo man, Michael Davitt, the evicted peasant from Straide, close by Moore Hall. That fight was bound to come when Moore's warning and the warning of men like him was set at nought. What a change it has made! and what has been lost to Ireland!

Moore died in 1870. His last year of life saw a hope that Presbyterian farmers of the North, interested in Tenant Right, who had been temporarily allied to Catholics in the struggle for Disestablishment, might unite solidly with the Nationalists. Even the Protestant gentry afforded numerous supporters to Butt's Home Rule policy at its outset. But of this nothing serious came. The Land Act of 1870 was ineffective, and it seemed that, in spite of Fenianism, all would

go on as before. Throughout the seventies the landlord class was in undisturbed supremacy. Country
gentlemen still talked in good set phrase about " the
robbery of the Church "; in actual fact they were very
complacently and competently helping to administer
its new constitution. Agriculture was prosperous and
rents went high, though the harsh and overbearing
landlord was condemned by his fellows. This, however, was poor consolation to the tenants.   In the
county where I was brought up, one landlord was a
name of terror, and there was no redress from his
tyranny, until at last the peasantry found it for themselves. The grim old man died fighting hard before
his brains were dashed out on the roadside, and two
innocent people were killed along with him; but no
sane person could fail to perceive that, within five
years of his taking off, the whole district was improved
out of knowledge. The moral to be drawn was only
too obvious; yet none of the landlords drew it; the
established interest of a class is too strong a thing for
that class to shake themselves out of its influence.

The men of that generation—how well I remember
them! most vividly perhaps as they used to come in
to church on Sunday morning, when the ladies of their
families addressed themselves to devotions kneeling,
while the men said their prayers standing, peering
mysteriously into their tall hats—a strange ritual, of
which traces may be observed at the House of Com-
mons, but nowhere else, I fancy, on earth. On week
days they lived an orderly, dignified existence in their
big old-fashioned houses, leaving home little, though
the more cultivated among them had travelled in their
youth and knew thoroughly some foreign country. In

their own orbit they had power, leisure, and defer-
ence, all of which set a stamp upon them; individuality
had great scope to develop, and an able man among
them was a man made for government.   One such
stands out in my memory.   Stormy tales were told of
his youth, but from himself no one heard a whisper of
these far-off exploits; small, exquisitely neat, finely
made and finely featured, he was courteous and gentle-
spoken with all; but he was of those quiet creatures
who breed fear.   I cannot imagine the situation of
power of responsibility from which he would have
shrunk, or to which he would have been unequal;
neither can I imagine him anxious in the pursuit of
office.   That was Parnell's type.   Parnell's strength
appears to have lain precisely in that self-confidence
which was a law to itself and which no prestige of
fame or authority could shake or overawe.   The men
who might have been Ireland's leaders were men
extraordinarily suited for the conduct of affairs, but as
a class they had been thrown out of their natural relation.   Castlereagh, who in his cold efficiency had
much in common with Parnell, accomplished a desperate deed when he made the Union through them.   He
committed their honour to justify for all time that
transaction.   If those who condemned the Union were
not traitors, then the class from whom it was bought
with cash and titles stood convicted of infamy; and
since the heart of Ireland loathed and detested Castlereagh's work, the whole body of the Irish gentry found
themselves inevitably estranged from the heart of Ireland.   On one side was the interest of a class—and
not merely the material interest but the interest of its
honour, which sought a justification in the name of

loyalty; on the other was the interest of Ireland; and the landlord who chose the side of Ireland severed himself necessarily, as Moore had to do, from his own friends and kin.

For years now there has been moving through many minds in Ireland the question whether this state of things must permanently endure.   Is that estrangement inevitable? I at least think otherwise. Throughout the last two decades of the nineteenth century landlord and tenant were opposed in a struggle for definite material interests; it was a fight not only for free conditions of tenure but for the reduction of rent, if not for its total abolition.   A way of peace was found in State-aided land purchase, and in a reconstitution of the whole agricultural order.   The landlords, where they have been bought out, have not even the duty of rent collecting.   How will this affect their traditional attitude, which calls itself loyalty to the English connexion, but which I interpret rather as a traditional justification of the Union and of the hereditary landlord policy? If self-government is established without dissolution of the Union, is it not reasonable to suppose that there will be a change in men's dispositions?

The question involved is really more serious, though of far less political importance, than that of Ulster. Whatever happens, the industrial community of Belfast and its district is not going to run away.   That element will not be lost to Ireland; it is too strong, too well able to assert itself; and it is anchored by its interest.   The ex-landlords, now that their occupation is gone, are bound to Ireland only by habit and attachment.   At present they fulfil no essential function;

and it will be open undoubtedly for the gentry once
more to make an error mischievous to Ireland and
disastrous to themselves. They may take up the line
of unwilling submission, of refusal to co-operate, of
cold-shouldering and crying down the new Parliament
and the new Ministry. Social pressure may be exercised to keep men from seeking election, and so to
perpetuate the existing severance between the leisured
and wealthier classes and the main body of the nation.
There will be strong tendencies in this direction. But
on the other hand I think that among the men who
have grown up under the new order there is an increas-
ing willingness to accept the change. One friend of
mine—no politician, and, like all non-politicians, a
Unionist—said to me lately that he would be rather
disappointed if Home Rule did not become law—he
was "curious about it"; and he added, "I think a
great many like me have the same feeling." Others
probably have a more positive outlook, and desire to
take an active part in the public life of their country;
and there will be a strong desire among Irish Nationalists to bring in at the outset those who wish to come
in. On the other hand, no less certainly, there will be
the feeling that is natural towards those who wish to
reap where they have not sown; and the gentry will
need to make allowance for this. If they set out with
the notion, as some did when Local Government was
established, that places are theirs by right when they
condescend to take them—that they are entitled to
election because they have more money, more education, because, if you will, they are, in the eye of pure
reason, better qualified—nothing but trouble can come
of such a disposition. Ireland, which in George Henry

Moore's time was the most aristocratically governed part of the British Isles, is now by far more democratic, at all events, than England : the poor man is on a level with the rich, and means to stay there. Those who want to go into Irish politics, under Home Rule as now, must take their chances in the ruck; but if they do, they will find a people ready and even eager to recognise their qualities, and to allot perhaps more consideration than is due to their social position.

With all their practical democracy, the Irish have a great tenderness for "the old stock." In the cases (and there are many hundreds of them) where a landlord or professional man or Protestant clergyman has been for long years a real friend and support and counsellor to his poorer neighbours, as Irish in voice and looks and gesture as they, sharing their tastes and their aversions, their sport and their sorrow, yet divided and cut off from them by a kind of political religion, I believe from my heart that there will be on both sides a willingness to celebrate the end of that old discord in some happy compact. But on both sides there must be generosity and a sympathy with natural hesitations and reluctances. Whatever comes or goes, the old domination of the gentry has disappeared; yet, whatever comes or goes, men of that class may find a sphere of usefulness and even of power in Ireland. But this will be infinitely easier to achieve when the great subject of contention is removed, and when the ex-landlord can seek election, and the ex-tenant can support him, without a sense on either side of turning against the traditional loyalties of a class.

1913.

YESTERDAY IN IRELAND

"OH, maybe it was yesterday, or forty years ago," says the verse of an Irish song. That is the kind of indeterminate "yesterday" which is described in *Irish Memories* by two friends who have made some memories of Ireland imperishable. "The Ireland that Martin and I knew when we were children," writes Miss Somerville, "is fast leaving us; every day some landmark is wiped out." No one knows better than she that while in many parts of Ireland you must go back very close on forty years to reach any likeness of that old way of life, yet in other parts yesterday and forty years ago are very much the same. Still, she would reply, and I must admit, that one profound modification has affected even the most unchanging places, altering the whole position of the class in which she was born and bred. In a sense, all her memories of Ireland concern themselves with this change, depicting either what formerly was, and the process of its passing, or what yet remains and seems likely to vanish too. Her presentment of yesterday is well worth study, for its outlook is typical of the most generous and shrewdest minds among the Irish gentry. I use here an old-fashioned word, somewhat decried, but it is the only one that expresses my meaning.

But readers will know that this is not only a book of memories; it is, if not a memoir, at least the memorial of a singularly brilliant Irish woman.   Miss Somerville had planned to write her recollections, as she had written so much else, in collaboration with her cousin and comrade, " Martin Ross "—Miss Violet Martin, of Ross, in County Galway. It did not so fall out; and though in this volume one is aware that the narrator is often (by a sort of sub-conscious habit) speaking out of two minds, from a dual complex of associations, and though considerable fragments of Martin Ross's own writing give a justification to the joint signature, yet one of the two comrades is joint author now only in so far as she is part of all the memories, and a surviving influence little likely to pass away.   But her stock, so to say, in the partnership remains; Galway, no less than Cork, is the field over which these memories travel.   In the main, the book is concerned with recalling the joint kindred of the two friends and cousins, and reconstituting the surroundings and the atmosphere of both families. Families, however, are conceived and depicted in their most extended relations; figures are evoked of chief, vassal, page and groom, tenant and master; and with them go their '' opposite numbers '' (to borrow an army term) from chieftainess to cook.   Chieftainesses are there unmistakably.   One ex-beauty had retired from the Court of the Regent to Castle Townshend (Miss Somerville's personal background), and there lived long, '' noted for her charm of manner, her culture and her sense of humour.''

Near the end of her long life she went to the funeral of a relative, leaning decorously upon the arm of a kinsman.   At the churchyard a countryman pushed forward between her and the coffin. She thereupon disengaged her arm from that of her squire and struck the countryman in the face.

Miss Somerville observes that such stories may help to explain the French Revolution; but she adds, quite plausibly :—

> It is no less characteristic of the time that the countryman's attitude does not come into the story, but it seems to me probable that he went home and boasted then, and for the rest of his life, that old Madam ———— had " bet him in a blow in the face."

Undoubtedly the chieftain-spirit is admired, and not least when it shows itself in a woman.   A more lenient and more modern example is to be found in the account of a dispute about bounds in a transaction under the Land Purchase Act.   After all other agencies failed, the landlord's sister called the disputants before her to the disputed spot, stepped the distance of the land debatable, drove her walking-stick into a crevice of the rock (disputes are passionate in opposite ratio to the value of the land) and, collecting stones, built a small cairn round it.   " Now men," she said, " in the name of God let this be the bounds." And it was so.   " It failed the agent, and it failed the landlord, and it failed the priest; but Lady Mary settled it," was the summing up of one of the disputants.   That was a chieftainess for you.

Not inferior in chieftainly spirit was Martin Ross's grandfather who " had the family liking for a horse."

> It is recorded that in a dealer's yard in Dublin he mounted a refractory animal, in his frock-coat and tall hat, and took him round St. Stephen's Green at a gallop, through the traffic, laying into him with his umbrella.

Somehow that picture gives a measure of the remoteness.   Stephen's Green was not then a place of square-set granite pavement, tram-rails and large swift-moving electric trams; it was a leisurely promenade where large slow-moving country gentlemen turned out in tall hats and frock-coats. We of Miss Somerville's generation depend on our imagination, not on memory, to reconstruct the scene. The grandfather in question died before the great famine of 1847, which shook and in many places uprooted the old order without yet bringing in the new. His son, Martin Ross's father, had the famine to cope with and survived it; but of the second convulsion from which emerged the Ireland of to-day he saw only the beginning, for he died in 1873, when the organised peasant uprising was at most a menace. But his wife knew both periods—the bad times of the late 'forties and the bad times of the early eighties. The true link with the past for the writers of *Irish Memories* is through the female line. This is a book of mothers and daughters rather than of fathers and sons.

Martin Ross's mother went back easily in memory to the society which had known the Irish Parliament, had made or accepted the Union, and which, after the Union, exercised chieftainship in Ireland. She was the daughter of Chief Justice Bushe, one of Grattan's rivals in oratory, who, like Grattan, had opposed the Union with all the resources of his eloquence. Against his name in the private Castle list of voters for the crucial division had been written in despair one word: "Incorruptible." He was the common ancestor whose blood made the bond of kinship between Miss Somerville and Martin Ross, and both these staunch Unionist ladies are passionately proud of the part which their grandfather played in resisting the Union; just as you will find the staunchest Ulster Covenanters exulting in the fact that they had a forbear " out " with the United Irishmen at Antrim or Ballynahinch in 1798. No wonder Englishmen find Ireland puzzling; but Scots understand, for their own records abound in examples of the same para- doxes of historic sentiment.

Yesterday in Ireland, I think, for my present pur- pose comes to define itself as the period between the famine of 1847 and the famine of 1879—between the downfall of O'Connell and Parnell's coming to power. We who were born in the 'sixties grew up in the close of it, and perhaps recognise now more clearly than when they were with us the characters of our kindred who were a part of it as mature human beings. " The men and women, but more specially the women of my mother's family and generation, are a lost pattern, a vanished type." I could say the same as Miss Somerville. There was a spaciousness about those people, a disregard of forms and conventions, a habit of thinking and acting for themselves which really came down from a long tradition of interpreting the law to their own liking. Miss Somerville and her comrade knew the type in its fullest development, for both grew up in far-out Atlantic-bordering regions— Carbery of West Cork, Connemara of West Galway— where the countryside knew scarcely " any inhabitants but the gentry and their dependents. 'Where'd we be at all if it wasn't for the Colonel's Big Lady?' said the hungry country-women, in the Bad Times, scurry- ing, barefooted, to her in any emergency to be fed and doctored and scolded." So writes Miss Somer- ville of her mother; so might Martin Ross have written of her father, who was, so far as in him lay, a Provi- dence for his tenantry. Yet there is a story told of

Mr. Martin that throws a flood of light on the whole position of affairs.   Who were indeed the dependents? And on what did they depend?   The story tells of a widow down by Lough Corrib, long in arrears with her rent.

The Master sent to her two or three times, and in the end he walked down himself, after his breakfast, and he took Thady (the steward) with him.   Well, when he went into the house, she was so proud to see him, and "Your Honour is welcome," says she, and she put a chair for him.   He didn't sit down at all, but he was standing up there with his back to the dresser, and the children were sitting down one side the fire.   The tears came from the Master's eyes, Thady seen them fall down the cheek.   "Say no more about the rent," says the Master to her, "you need say no more about it till I come to you again."   Well, it was the next winter, men were working in Gurthnamuckla and Thady with them, and the Master came to the wall of the field, and a letter in his hand, and he called Thady over to him.   What had he to show but the widow's rent that her brother in America sent her.

Martin Ross, writing in the light of to-day, makes this comment :—

It will not happen again; it belongs to an almost forgotten régime, that was capable of abuse, yet capable too of summoning forth the best impulses of Irish hearts.

War, famine and pestilence—all these are capable of summoning forth splendid impulses; but society should not be organised to give play to these hazards of feeling.   The fundamental truth about yesterday in Ireland is that everybody accepted as natural a state of affairs under which Irish gentry were taking rents that could not be earned on the land which was burdened with them.   Landlord and tenant alike were really dependent on what was sent back by the sons and daughters of poor people from America to prevent the break-up of homes.   The whole situation was false, from top to bottom. At top, a small class, physically and often mentally superb, full of charm, extraordinarily agreeable, fit for great uses, but by temperament, habit and education unequipped for its proper task of equipping and directing the labour out of which ultimately it had to live or perish. It perished. At bottom, a multitude with marvellous constitution, undermined by age-long under-feeding, friendly, most lovable, most winning, but untrained and unequipped, half-hearted in its business of rolling the pitiless stone up the never-ending hill. It survived —clinging with a desperate tenacity to the soil which so meagrely nourished it. But during that generation of yesterday—and how many generations before it?— there grew up inevitably, from the conditions, a traditional toleration of incompetence, a faith as it were in inefficiency. Ireland of yesterday was bound up in one vicious circle of work that was necessarily underpaid because it was inefficient, and work that was necessarily inefficient because it was underpaid. In the lower class there were no reserves; the dependants lived from hand to mouth, and when hand failed to find food, they had to come to the upper class, first for remission of its claims on them and then for actual subsistence. But the dependence was mutual, and there were no reserves at top equal to the needs of that joint hazard. Penury was only at two removes from the "gentry houses." While the first line of defence, the tenants, held good, the world went pleasantly for the Ireland of yesterday. But when that line broke, and starvation burst in, then the best men and women in the big houses flung their all into the common stock, and went under—as did the chief of the Martins in Connemara.

That, however, happened the day before
yesterday; yesterday saw nothing so dire.   But
the menace of it was always there, and the
rest of Ireland gradually consolidated itself for a
struggle to win what had long ago been acquired for
Protestant Ulster—the right of a tenant to what his
own labour created.   The Ulster custom has done for
Ulster, industrial as well as agricultural, more than is
generally perceived.   It gave in some degree recognition to efficiency.   Tenure was there less precarious,
less dependent on the landlord's pleasure; men were
freer, work had more rights.   There was less room for
impulse, perhaps less appeal to affection; but when a
business relation is based on impulse and affection,
where rights are not solid and defined, the sense of
obligation easily leads men astray.   That which is
given out of loyalty and affection comes to be taken
as a due.   Martin Ross—" Miss Violet," whom the
people of Ross called " the gentle lady," as beautiful
a name as was ever earned by mortal—inherited with
little qualification the landlord standpoint.   She recalls
the story of an election in 1872, when her father, going
to vote in Oughterard, saw " a company of infantry
keeping the way for Mr. Arthur Guinness (afterwards
Lord Ardilaun) as he conveyed to the poll a handful
of his tenants to vote for Captain Trench, he himself
walking in front with the oldest of them on his arm."
She does not ask if the tenants desired to be so conveyed.   She merely describes how her father " ranged
through the crowd incredulously, asking for this or
that tenant, unable to believe that they had deserted
him."   When he came home, " even the youngest
child of the house could see how great had been the

blow. It was not the political defeat, severe as that
was, it was the personal wound, and it was incur-
able."

Looking back through all those years, the "gentle
lady" can see nothing in that episode but a case of
priestly intimidation.   "One need not blame the
sheep who passed in a frightened huddle from one
fold to another." Yet friends of mine in Galway look
back on it in a very different spirit; they remember
the Nolan-Trench election and Captain Nolan's victory as a triumph of the poor, a first instalment of
freedom; it brought with it an exultation very different
from the mere outburst of hatred that these pages
suggest. What is more, having been privileged to sit
in the most widely representative assembly of Irishmen that modern Ireland has known, I can testify that
to-day peer and peasant, clergy and laymen, those
who opposed it, and those others who fought for it,
alike admit that the change which such a victory fore-
shadowed was necessary and was beneficent. But it
was a revolution. Ireland of yesterday was Ireland
before the revolution. The Ireland that Miss Somerville and Martin Ross have lived in as grown women
has been a country in the throes of a revolution, long
drawn-out, with varying phases, yet still incomplete.
Those who judge Ireland should remember this.   In
time of revolution, life is difficult, ancient loyalties
clash with new yet living principles, sympathy and
justice even are unsure guides. No country could have
been kept for forty years in such a ferment as Ireland
has known without profound demoralisation.   We
may well envy those who lived more easily and
quietly in the Ireland of yesterday, and held with an

H

unquestioning spirit to the state of things in which
they were born.

Such were the folk of whom Miss Somerville writes
with "that indomitable family pride that is an asset
of immense value in the history of a country." They
"took all things in their stride without introspection
or hesitation.   Their unflinching conscientiousness,
their violent church-going (I speak of the sisters), were
accompanied by a whole-souled love of a spree and a
wonderful gift for a row."   I can corroborate her
details, especially the last.   All those that I recall had
some talent for feuds; at least, in every family there
would be one warrior, male or female; and all had
the complete contempt, not so much for convention
as for those who were affected in their lives (or cos-
tumes) by any standard that was not home-made.   But
in all humility I must admit that the real heroines of
this book—Mrs. Somerville and Mrs. Martin—outshine
anything that my memory can produce.   When
Martin Ross and her mother went back to West Galway and re-established themselves at their old home,
a letter from her to Miss Somerville describes one
incident :—

I wish you had seen Paddy Griffy, a very active little old man,
and a beloved of mine, when he came down on Sunday night to
welcome me.   After the usual hand-kissings on the steps, he put
his hands over his head and stood in the doorway, I suppose invok-
ing his saint.   He then rushed into the hall.
"Dance, Paddy," screamed Nurse Bennett (my foster-mother,
now our maid-of-all-work).
And he did dance, and awfully well, too, to his own singing.
Mamma, who was attired in a flowing pink dressing-gown and a
black hat trimmed with lilac, became suddenly emulous, and with
her spade under her arm joined in the jig.   This lasted for about
a minute, and was a never-to-be-forgotten sight.   They skipped
round the hall, they changed sides, they swept up to each other and
back again and finished with the deepest curtseys.

My own mother would gladly have done the same on a like occasion, but she lacked Mrs. Martin's talent for the jig. Mrs. Somerville is sketched with a free and humorous hand. I quote only one detail, but it shows the real Irishwoman, more deeply in touch with Ireland's traditional life than any Gaelic League could bring her. Question arose how to find a suitable offering for ' an old servant of forty years' standing, whose fancies were few and her needs none.' " Give her a nice shroud," said Mrs. Somerville, " there's nothing in the world she'd like so well as that."

Shakespeare could not have outdone that intuition, and only one of the larger breed would have been unconventional enough to suggest what the younger generation, hampered by other feelings than those of West Carbery, " were too feeble to accept."

These two traits belong to the harmonious and thoroughly Irish grouping in which such ladies as Mrs. Martin and Mrs. Somerville were central figures of the whole countryside. That grouping exists no longer, and this book has to describe the discord which interrupted that harmony. Martin Ross's elder brother, Robert Martin (famous in his day as the writer and singer of *Ballyhooly,* and a score of other topical songs), left his work as a London journalist to help in fighting the first campaign which brought the word " boycott " into usage.

It was at this work (his sister writes), that Robert knew for the first time what it was to have every man's hand against him, to meet the stare of hatred, the jeer and the sidelong curse ; to face endless drives on outside cars with his revolver in his hand ; to plan the uphill tussle with boycotted crops and cattle for which a market could scarcely be found ; to know the imminence of death,

when by accidentally choosing one of two roads he evaded the man
with a gun who had gone out to wait for him.

Robert Martin faced, in a word, the earliest and
ugliest phases of that Irish revolution, which was the
Nemesis of the all too easy and too pleasant ways of
yesterday in Ireland. Later, after his death, Martin
Ross herself had to gain some experience of the same
trouble. When she went back with her mother to
re-establish the family home from which they had
been fifteen years absent, there was a hostile element
in the parish, and gracious hospitality was ungra-
ciously met. An attempt was made to keep children
from a children's party which she had organised. The
move was half-hearted and her energy defeated it, but
that the attempt should be made was such " a facer "
as she had never before known. Like many another
ugly thing in Ireland, it originated in that cowardly
fear of public opinion which is to be found on the
seamy side of all revolutions; and it did not stand
against her " gallant fight to restore the old ways, the
old friendships."

The old ways, in so far as they meant the old
friendships, she might hope to restore, although the
friendship would, half consciously, take on a new
accent; personality would count for more in it, position for less. But the old relation which authorised
a kind-hearted landlord to feel that his tenants had
" deserted him " because they voted against his wish
in an election—that is gone for ever; and gone, at all
events, for the present, is the local leadership of the
gentry.

I question whether it is realised that in parting from
that leadership Ireland lost what was in a sense Home

Rule. In the " yesterday " of which I write Ireland was governed in all its parochial and most intimate affairs by a class or a caste; but that governing class was Irish—Irish with a limitation, no doubt. yet still indisputably Irish. When that rule perished, when that class lost its local ascendancy, government became the bastard compromise that we have known, with power inharmoniously divided between official-dom and agitators. The law was framed and admini-stered by officials, often English or Scotch, possessing no authority except what the law conferred on them. Authority lay very largely with popular leaders; but leadership and authority alike were purely personal, depending on a man's own qualities and the support which they evoked. No man was born to it as of right, and such authority is far more precarious than the established power of a governing class. This is a weakness in all democratically-governed countries, but where there is self-government, the individual, in entering upon office, acquires the support and the prestige of a long-established machinery of power. He ceases to be merely the individual when he becomes part of the Government. For the Irish leaders this reinforcement to the personal authority has never existed; they have been at a terrible dis-advantage as compared with all other democratic poli-ticians; and consequently the power exercised by them has always, except perhaps at Parnell's zenith, been far less than was the combined authority of the gentry before the landlord rule was broken. Those who shared in that authority acted, and could afford to act, with unquestioning confidence; they were surer of themselves, than is any popular leader or any offi-

cial in Ireland of to-day. It seldom occurred to them
to ask whether their conduct in any juncture might
meet with approval; being a law to other people, they
were naturally a law to themselves, and an Irish law.
Their power was excessive, and demoralised them by
its lack of limitation; yet many of the qualities which
it bred, made them an element of great value in the
country. These qualities are by no means extinct in
their kindred, nor is the tradition of their right to
leadership forgotten.

Of one thing Miss Somerville and those for whom
she speaks (she is a real spokeswoman) may be well
assured. Whatever be the surface mood of the
moment, whatever the passing effect of war's hectic
atmosphere, nothing is more deeply realised throughout Ireland than the need to restore the old ways, the
old friendships—the need to bring back the gentry to
their old uses in Ireland, and to so much of leadership
as should be theirs by right of fitness. When the history of the Irish Convention comes to be fully recorded,
it will be seen that a great desire was universally felt,
cordially uttered, in that assembly, to bridge over the
gulf which divides us from yesterday in Ireland, and
to recover for the future much of what was admirable,
valuable and lovable in a past that is not unkindly
remembered. Indeed, it is plain that Miss Somerville has felt the influences that were abroad on the
winds, when she wrote of her comrade :—

Her love of Ireland, combined with her distrust of some of those
newer influences in Irish affairs to which her letters refer, made
her dread any weakening of the links that bind the United King-
dom into one; but I believe that if she were here now, and saw
the changes that the past eighteen months have brought to Ireland, she would be quick to welcome the hope that Irish politics

are lifting at last out of the controversial rut of centuries, and that although it has been said of East and West that " never the two shall meet," North and South will yet prove that in Ireland it is always the impossible that happens.

North and South—that is a more difficult gulf to bridge, for the one I have been speaking of is only a breach to repair.   But industrial Protestant Ulster and the rest of Ireland have never really been one.   Unity there has not to be re-established, but created. Martin Ross went to the North only once " at the tremendous moment of the signing of the Ulster Covenant," and she was profoundly impressed by what she saw.   She wrote about it publicly and she wrote also privately (in a letter which I had the honour to receive) a passage well worth quoting :—

I did not know the North at all.   What surprised me about the place was the feeling of cleverness and go, and also the people struck me as being hearty.   If only the South would go up North and see what they are doing there, and how they are doing it, and ask them to show them how, it would make a good deal of difference.   And then the North should come South and see what nice people we are, and how we do that.

When that reciprocal pilgrimage was accomplished by the Convention, her anticipations were more than justified.   But how clever she was !   In a flash, she, coming there a stranger, hits on the word which describes Ulster and differentiates it from the rest of Ireland.   " Hearty," that is what they are; it is the good side of their self-content.   No people that is in revolution can be hearty—least of all when revolution has dragged on through more than a generation.   Distrust of your comrades—distrust of your leaders—self-distrust—these are the characteristic vices of revolution (look at Russia), and they sow a bitter seed.   Pro-

testant Ulster has never known revolution; for it yesterday and to-day have been happily, naturally, continuous. Political change it has known, normal and
beneficent; land purchase came to Ulster as a by-pro-
duct of what the rest of Ireland endured in torment,
and agony, and self-mutilation. Clever the Northerns
are, but their cleverness issues prosperously in action;
they carry on in a solidly-established order; they have
not needed to break down before they could begin to
build. That is why their heartiness stood out when
they were assembled, as I have seen them in a common
council of Irishmen, which was also, thank heaven,
a companionship. But the world at large can see it
exhibited in another way. Contrast the work of the
Ulster Players with that of the Abbey Theatre. *The
Drone* is perhaps not the best of new Irish comedies,
but it is infinitely the pleasantest; there is no bitter
tang in its hearty humour. Even in *The Enthusiast*,
a sketch which has some touch of pessimism, there is
little more than a good-humoured shrug of the
shoulders when the Enthusiast abandons his pretensions to make himself heard against the banging of
Orange drums. I find a very different note, not
merely in the work of Synge, of Boyle, Colum, Len-
nox Robinson, and the rest of the Abbey dramatists,
but even in the books of which Miss Somerville was
joint author. When Ireland is seen with the eyes, for
instance, of her Major Yeates, is not the whole attitude one of amused and acquiescent resignation? Take
the hunting out of it (with all the humours of the
hunt)—take the shooting and fishing—and what is left
but a life (to borrow a phrase from Mr. George Moore)
" as melancholy as bog-water and as ineffectual."

YESTERDAY IN IRELAND 113

Miss Somerville would probably decline to imagine an Ireland with these unthinkable suppressions, but after all, we cannot live by or for sport alone. What gave dignity and reality to the life of yesterday was leadership in one class, and loyalty in the other. Leadership resting on ownership is gone now, dead as the dodo; what is left for the like (say) of Mr. Flurry Knox if he should begin to take himself seriously? You can easily make a soldier of him; we have all met him in trenches and observed his airy attitude in No Man's Land. But soldiering has generally meant expatriation. For my part, I hope some day to see this gentleman (or his like) play a useful part in some battalion of Irish territorials—some home service offshoot of the Connaught Rangers. But that is not enough. If those who, like Miss Somerville, love Ireland's yesterday and desire to link it up with a worthy to-morrow, there must be a wider understanding of Ireland, not in the North only, but in that element of the South and West which stands to-day in a sense morally expatriated. The Irish gentry who complain that their tenants " deserted " them must learn where they themselves failed their tenants. Leadership cannot depend merely on a power to evict, and they would to-day repudiate the desire for a leadership so grounded. But between free men where there is not comprehension there can be no leadership.

I take first what is most difficult—the very heart of antagonism. Everyone who desires to understand Ireland to-day should read Patrick Pearse's posthumous book, called boldly *The Story of a Success*

1 " The Story of a Success." By P. H. Pearse. Being a Record of St. Erda's College, September, 1908, to Easter, 1916. Edited by Desmond Ryan, B.A. Maunsel & Co.

It is the spiritual history of Pearse's career as a schoolmaster, edited and completed by his pupil, Desmond
Ryan; and it is a book by which no one can be justly
offended—a book instinct with nobility, chivalry and
high courtesy, free from all touch of bitterness; a book,
too, shot through and slashed with that tragic irony
which the Greeks knew to be the finest thrill in literature—the word spoken, to which the foreknown event
gives an echo of double meaning. Pearse was concerned with Ireland's yesterday; he desired to bring
the present and the future into organic rotation with
the past. But his yesterday was not Miss Somerville's
nor mine. The son of an English mechanic and a
Galway woman, he was brought up in Connemara
after the landlord power had ceased to exist. Ireland's
past for him and Irish tradition were seen through the
medium of an imagination in touch only with the peasant life, but inspired by books and literature, written
and spoken. His yesterday was of no definite past,
for he had been born in a revolution when the immediate past was obliterated. In his vision a thousand
years were no more than the watch of some spell-
bound chivalry, waiting for the voice that should say,
" It is the time." Cuchulain and Robert Emmet were
his inspirations, but the champion of the legendary
Red Branch cycle and the young revolutionary of
Napoleon's days were near to him one as the other, in
equally accessible communion. Going back easily to
the heroic legends, on which, though blurred in their
outline, his boyhood had been fostered by tellers of
long-transmitted tales at a Connemara hearthside, he
found the essential beauty and significance where
more learned though less cultured readers have been

bewildered by what seemed to them wild extravagances of barbarism. What he gathered from them
did not lie inert, but quickened in him and in others,
for he was the revolutionary as schoolmaster—the
most drastic revolutionary of all. In the school review
which was the first vehicle for these writings of his, he
hoped to found " the rallying point for the thought and
aspirations of all those who would bring back again
in Ireland that Heroic Age which reserved its highest
honour for the hero who had the most childlike heart,
for the king who had the largest pity, and for the poet
who visioned the truest image of beauty." All his
theory of education was based on the old Irish institution of fosterage, which was no mere physical tie of
the breast; the child sent to be fostered was sent to be
bred and trained, and it was a tie stronger than that
of its blood or of the breast. *Irish Memories* shows
incidentally how great a part this fosterage played in
the Ross of yesterday—that family with its multitude
of children was bound to the countryside by all the
" Nursies." But the Martin household, and all similar
households were, in a less literal sense, fostered by
the peasantry at large. The truest part of education
should be to know your own country (a principle much neglected in Ireland), and which of us all,
who had the good fortune to be brought up in touch
with Irish peasant life, does not realise our debt? We
received a devotion, an affection, for which no
adequate return could be made—it is the nature of
fosterage that the fosterer should give more than can
ever be requited; but we gained also our real knowledge, in so far as we ever had it, of the countryside,
the traditional wisdom, the inherited way of life.

There was more to be got if we had the wit to assimilate it. Almost all of modern Irish literature that has
lasting value is evoked from elements floating in
peasant memory, in the peasant mind, and in the
coloured peasant speech of an Ireland which keeps
unbroken descent from a long line of yesterdays. Mr.
Yeats is only the chief of those who draw from this
source. Miss Somerville herself and her cousin must
have known well that the real worth of their work lies
in their instinct for the poetry which, more specially
in Gaelic-speaking regions, sits in rags by roadside and
chimney corner. Irish poetry is not only the tragic
voice of the keene; Gaelic had its comic muse as well,
a robust virago, of the breed which produced Aristophanes and Rabelais—and Slipper with his gift for
epic narrative is a camp-follower of that regiment.

Yet in Miss Somerville's appreciation there is often
—not always—a sense of the incongruity as well as of
the beauty in peasant speech. The woman crying for
alms of bread who described her place of habitation,
"I do be like a wild goose over on the side of Dro-
minidy Wood," moves to laughter as well as to pity
with the dignity of her phrase. Ireland so felt is Ireland perceived from the outside—seen as a picturesque
ruin. You cannot so see Pearse; he is too strong for
even compassionate laughter. What he embodies is
the central strength of Irish nationalism—its disregard
of the immediate event.

Wise men have told me that I ought never to set my foot on a
path unless I can see clearly whither it will lead me. But that
philosophy would condemn most of us to stand still till we rot.
Surely one can do no more than assure one's self that each step
one takes is right; and as to the rightness of a step one is fortunately answerable only to one's conscience and not to the wise men

of the counting house.   The street will pass judgment on our enter-
prises according as they have " succeeded " or " failed." But if
one can feel that one has striven faithfully to do a right thing, does
not one stand ultimately justified, no matter what the issue of one's
attempt, no matter what the sentence of the street?

By such teaching he commended to his scholars,
and to Ireland, the spirit which he desired to see
expressed in " that laughing gesture of a young man
that is going into battle or climbing to a gibbet."
Strange country, that has the gibbet always before the
eyes and almost before the aspiration of its idealists!
It was so yesterday—in all the yesterdays—and yet
the reason is plain.   All the aspirations of such
idealists have been regarded as criminal by the class
for which Miss Somerville and her cousin speak—
criminal and menacing to those who, holding the
power, arrogated to themselves a monopoly of loyalty.
They have always conceived of Pearse and his like as
thirsting for their blood.   Miss Edgeworth, in a letter
printed for the first time in *Irish Memories*, writes :—
" I fear our throats will be cut by order of O'Connell
and Co. very soon."   We know enough to-day about
O'Connell to realise how far this estimate lay from the
truth of things; yet Miss Somerville herself talks about
" Parnell and his wolf-pack."   Justin McCarthy, John
Redmond, Willie Redmond—these were some of the
wolves who presumably wanted to tear Miss Somerville's kindred to pieces.   That is where the change
must come; there must be among the gentry some
generous understanding of Nationalist leaders before
the grave has closed over them.   Anyone can see
what is bad in Sinn Féin, but no one can fight that
evil effectively, no one can convert to better uses the

ill-guided force which Sinn Féin represents, until he understands what is best in it. Sinn Féin has largely replaced a movement which, in its later phases, dwelt perhaps too much on the material advantages which it offered as the reward of support. Sinn Fein's strength has lain not in what it has offered, but in what it has asked; it has asked for devotion, and Pearse certainly both gave that and received it. Such was his teaching, and I do not know a better saying for the Irish gentry to ponder over than the last sentence in these essays of his : " The highest thing anyone can do is to serve."

That temper was perhaps lacking in the Ireland of yesterday which Miss Somerville so lovingly describes. To command loyalty as a right, to reward it by generosity, by indulgence—this made part of the ideal of leadership; but scarcely to be laborious either in rendering or exacting capable work.

The old way of life was good for children, as Martin Ross describes it in her sketch of her brother's upbringing.

> Everything in those early days of his was large and vigorous; tall trees to climb, great winds across the lake to wrestle with, strenuous and capable talk upstairs and downstairs, in front of furnaces of turf and logs, long drives and the big Galway welcome at the end of them.

But for the grown men, it lacked one thing : effort. Pleasant it was; lots of everything, lots of hunting, lots of game on the moors and bogs, lots of fish in lake and river, lots of beef and mutton on the farm, lots of logs and turf, lots of space—above all, lots of time, and always the spirit for a spree that made everyone " prefer good fun to a punctual dinner." There was only one deficiency : that way of life was apt to be short of cash. It was, in short, a life that could not pay its way. The "big Galway welcome" is just as big with a sounder economic system, that rests solidly on men's own work.   Anyone who knows Western Ireland can tell you that the quality of work is better on the land where men are their own masters than it was in the old days.   Yet even there we are not out of the old vicious circle of under-pay and under-work; and in the industrial life we are fully entangled in it.   But here also the revolutionary as schoolmaster has appeared. To my thinking the most momentous apparition in Ireland of our times is that of Mr. Ford, who is paying American wage rates for labour in Cork, and calculating, not to get value for his money at once, but to teach labour to be worth it. According to his gospel, as it was expounded to me, you will not get efficiency by offering to pay the wages of efficiency when labour becomes efficient: you must first provide the conditions of efficiency and then teach, just as in the army your first care is to get a recruit fit and your second to make him thorough in his ground work. That is the practical recognition of what yesterday in Ireland failed to recognise.

Nor does this ideal of strenuous and capable work exclude either the strenuous and capable talk of Martin Ross's Galway household or anything else that was excellent in the old way.   Certainly the most laborious and the most prosperous peasant household that I have ever known (and for many months I was part of it) was the most thoroughly and traditionally Irish, except that it was removed by one generation from Gaelic speech.   But the whole cast of mind was

Gaelic, remote as the poles from that " newer Ireland " which is in revolt against all tradition of authority—and, if they only knew it, against all Irish tradition.   Miss Somerville thinks, as a page in her book shows, that the newer Ireland has lost the endearing courtesy which is imposed by the genius of the Gaelic tongue, and is for that matter to be found in every line of Pearse's essays.   We can educate back to that without any detriment; we can be as efficient and as courteous as the Japanese.   Another thing is gone. Ireland of yesterday, even in its poverty, was a merry country; to-day, even in its prosperity, it is full of bitter, mirthless rancour and hate.   It will be a great thing if we can help to preserve for Ireland the exquisite benediction which a beggar woman in Skibbereen laid upon Martin Ross : " Sure, ye're always laughing!   That ye may laugh in the sight of the glory of Heaven."

1918.